Martin Wenzl

The creation of RB Leipzig

Authentic identity or self-deception?

Anchor Academic
Publishing

Wenzl, Martin: The creation of RB Leipzig. Authentic identity or self-deception?,
Hamburg, Anchor Academic Publishing 2016

Buch-ISBN: 978-3-96067-077-3
PDF-eBook-ISBN: 978-3-96067-577-8
Druck/Herstellung: Anchor Academic Publishing, Hamburg, 2016
Covermotiv: © pixabay.de

Bibliografische Information der Deutschen Nationalbibliothek:
Die Deutsche Nationalbibliothek verzeichnet diese Publikation in der Deutschen
Nationalbibliografie; detaillierte bibliografische Daten sind im Internet über
http://dnb.d-nb.de abrufbar.

Bibliographical Information of the German National Library:
The German National Library lists this publication in the German National Bibliography.
Detailed bibliographic data can be found at: http://dnb.d-nb.de

© Anchor Academic Publishing, Imprint der Diplomica Verlag GmbH
Hermannstal 119k, 22119 Hamburg
http://www.diplomica-verlag.de, Hamburg 2016
Printed in Germany

ACKNOWLEDGEMENT

The following pays a debt of gratitude to the people who have made the completion of this book possible. First I would like to thank my supervisor Associate Professor Georg Bouché who gave me helpful advice, supported me through his positive mood and had always an ear for my questions and needs.

On a more personal note, special thanks go to those closest to me. Thanks to my future wife Silke who prepared beside of her pregnancy every time a powerful meal which was necessary for the daily night shifts. She was of course my biggest supporter during the last years. Moreover, a great honour goes to my unborn son Lorenz who motivated me to fulfil my master degree and fight against procrastination. This in advance should be bridging the gap if he maybe comes into the same situation. Important to mention is the never ending support of my mother who has always believed in me since my beginning. In the critical period in which time came close to running out, I am also thankful to my mother in law Annemie who helped me out by taking over the daily walks with our dog Gaia.

I would also like to thank Helmut Schwendtner who had an eye on my phrasing and ideas. The correspondence with him helped to improve the consistency and coherence of the text. It shows me that he is a trustworthy friend despite the long distance. Thanks a lot to my brother Konrad who helped me distributing the survey in Nuremberg. Not to forget he was significantly involved in the evolvement of the topic itself. Through the regular chats about football and the slangy insert of "It would be interesting to know how the RBL fans see themselves", the idea of looking more closely at the issue began to come up.

Finally, I would like to dedicate my work to my father in law, Karlheinz Nieder who lost his fight against cancer within this spring.

EXECUTIVE SUMMARY

This book researches a five year old football club from Leipzig which was founded by Red Bull for marketing issues. Because the audience interest is surprisingly high the motivation for attendance of those fans has been investigated. To identify the degree of affiliation of Leipzig fans with the club also the SSIS have been examined. In a survey both online and at the stadium 223 football fans have been interviewed to give an opinion in regard to RB Leipzig. The result shows that the main reason for affiliation with the club is geographic first, aesthetics second and entertainment third. The SSIS shows that the affective factors are slightly more dominant than the cognitive factors. In combination with the high interest on club issues and the low distinction to rivals RBL fans show a typical characteristic of new team identification. A separate part of the survey demonstrates that opinions of football fans differs strongly trough their group belonging which is explainable with the SIT and SCT. In order to approach to the core topic the literature review considers sport sponsoring, identity based team brand management and team identification..

TABLE OF CONTENTS

LIST OF ABBREVIATIONS

BIRG	Bask in Reflected Glory
BSG	Betriebssportgemeinschaft
CBR	Customer Brand Relationship
CORF	Cut off Reflected Failure
CPI	Celebrity Performance Index
DFB	Deutscher Fußball Bund
DFL	Die Liga-Fußballverband
DIY	Do-It-Yourself
e.V.	eingetragener Verein
GDL	Goods-Dominant-Logic
GDR	German Democratic Republic
FAM	Fan Attendance Motivations
FC	Fußball-Club
FC	Football-Club
FIFA	Fédération Internationale de Football Association
GmbH	Gesellschaft mit beschränkter Haftung
MLB	Major League Baseball
MSC	Motivations of the Sport Consumer
MSSC	Motivation Scale for Sport Consumption
NBA	National Basketball Association
NFL	National Football League
NSL	National Soccer League
USA	United States of America
PAI	Points of Attachment Index
PCT	Psychological Commitment to Team
PSV	Philips Sport Vereniging
RB	Rasenballsport
RBL	Rasenballsport Leipzig
ROI	Return on Investment
SCT	Self-Categorization Theory
SDL	Service-Dominant-Logic
St.	Sankt

SFMS	Sport Fan Motivation Scale
SG	Sportgemeinschaft
SII	Sport Interest Inventory
SIT	Social Identity Theory
SSIS	Sport Spectator Identity Scale
SSV	Spiel- und Sport Verein
StDev	Standard Deviation
TAM	Team Association Management
UEFA	Union of European Football Associations
TSG	Turn- und Sportgemeinschaft
VfB	Verein für Bewegungsspiele
WNBA	Women's national basketball association

LIST OF FIGURES

LIST OF TABLES

1 INTRODUCTION

1.1 MOTIVATION

The FIFA World Cup 2014 is over and it is estimated that 3.2 billion people have watched at least one game during the last weeks.[1] In the end Germany won against Argentina after extra time in a tournament which takes place every four years. People all around the globe have witnessed a thrilling and dramatic final. The protagonist Bastian Schweinsteiger fought like a true warrior, stood up time and time again despite of the punishment he took by the Argentine defenders during the game.[2] Like a boxer in an epic battle, he tumbled, he fell, was given the count but in the end he stood triumphant. After he stemmed the golden trophy to the sky with a bloody cut under his right eye he was the ideograph of a hero.[3] This way of illustration serves a purpose in two ways. On the one hand people love to see that somebody is fighting hard for success; that enables sympathy and identification with the viewer's own self-concept. On the other hand when he reached his goals he created a wonder and the spectators were a part of it. The more he suffers the more he will be admired.[4] The events in sport and the athletes fulfil a wide range of functions for the society. They transport a kind of sense, social acknowledgement and the satisfaction of connection and identification.[5]

The huge interest in football combined with the staging of an event and the building up of players to heroes has attracted many companies for decades. Attracting interest and attention and selling parts of it to sponsors and advertisers is a lucrative business.[6] At the club level the dimension of partnerships with umbrella organizations or with football clubs is becoming greater year by year. The potential benefit through a partnership with professional clubs has transformed football from pure entertainment into a heavy competing business.[7]

But this development happened not due to the sport itself or the interaction with the audience. Some of the most important cases occurred in the 90´s and are mentioned here.

---

[1] cf. Teixeira, 2014
[2] cf. Fritsch, 2014
[3] cf. Spiller, 2014
[4] cf. Könecke, 2014, p.56-58
[5] cf. Könecke, 2014, p.67
[6] cf. Teixeira, 2014
[7] cf. Alexa, 2014, p.167

The deregulation of the player market which allows national football clubs in Europe to employ and field an unlimited number of foreign players (Bosman judgement). The introduction of additional competitions like the "Uefa Champions League" or the "Europa League" enables the best teams to compete more often against each other than before. This in consequence has created new means of income.[8] Moreover the central marketing of governing bodies[9] and the introducing of per-view combined with the stretching of the match schedule has pushed this tendency towards commercialisation even more.[10]

Against this background it's not amazing that the five biggest football leagues in Europe have recorded a steady growth in revenue for years. The professional football leagues in England, Germany, Spain, Italy and France combined achieve an astonishing revenue of 9.8 billion € in the season 2012/13. Furthermore the growth rate of revenue has averaged at 9.1% annually within the last 16 years.[11] This is one reason why football clubs and club associations are understood as private enterprises and brands.[12]

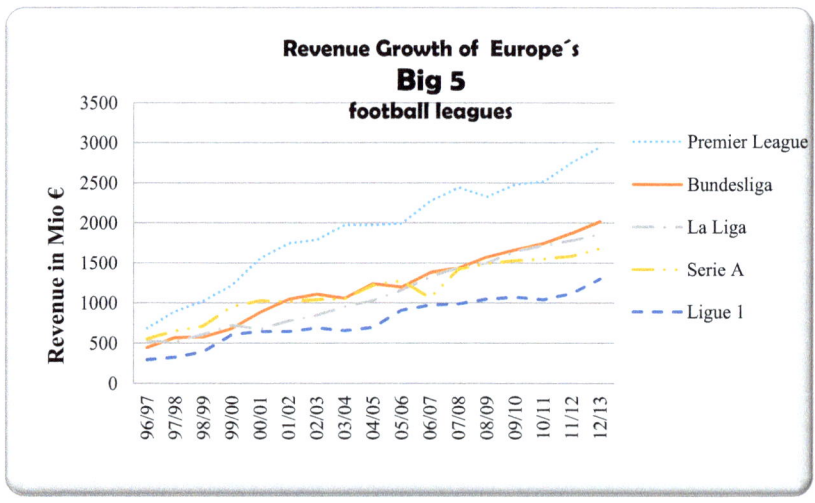

Figure 1.1 Revenue Growth of Europe´s Big 5 football leagues, own illustration

[8] cf. Schröer, 2009, p.11-12
[9] cf. Schröer, 2009, p.89
[10] cf. Schröer, 2009, p.63
[11] cf. Deloitte, 2014
[12] cf. Alexa, 2014, p.167

The importance of a strong brand and its credibility becomes relevant for long term contracts.[13] In the battle of selling licenses to sponsors and media worldwide the brand "Bundesliga" argues with several arguments. However the main argument is the huge stadium attendance. In comparison to other sport leagues the "Bundesliga" attracts the most people in Europe. With 41.914 spectators per match in the season 2012/2013 the first professional football league in Germany is outstanding.[14] But the gap between the English "premier league" and the German "Bundesliga" is getting smaller. In the season 2011/12 the difference add up nearly 10.000 spectators per match[15] but one year later the gap melted already down to 6.000 stadium viewers.[16]

Due to the rising knowledge about the advertising effectiveness many and huge investors are interested in participating in the football business.[17] But there is a significant difference to North-America where sport teams are franchise companies who have the entitlement to take part in the professional leagues. These companies can be sold, renamed and replaced to other cities which lead to several fan reactions.[18] In Germany such a form is forbidden by the governing body DFL. Even more the 50+1 law protects the clubs against losing the majority to an investor.[19] However clubs like Leverkusen who are sponsored by the pharmaceutical group Bayer and Wolfsburg who have the automobile company VW as a supporter are seen as artificially created clubs by many football supporters. In the youngest history another club Hoffenheim who gets supported by a huge company called SAP reached the first division. These football clubs have three things in common. They have a rich investor, a small supporter group and they are disliked by the common neutral sport fan. The so called test-tube clubs are infuriating the concurrence of the leagues. On the one hand they have a big advantage when buying players through the major donors and on the other hand they endanger the central selling argument of the brand "Bundesliga".[20]

---

[13] cf. Schilhaneck, 2006, p.286
[14] cf. DFL 2014, p.3
[15] cf. DFL 2013, p.8
[16] cf. DFL 2014, p.52
[17] cf. Teixeira, 2014
[18] cf. Roschmann, 2013, p.104
[19] cf. Schröer, 2013, p.204
[20] cf. Selldorf, 2013

Now a new "plastic club" is arising in Germany. Red Bull, the big partner, has created a professional club in Leipzig five years ago. The reaction of the fans and the other clubs are similar to the three clubs mentioned above. Furthermore RB Leipzig seems to polarize even more and various trial matches were aborted trough fan-movements.[21] On the 3rd of May 2014, the sponsored club from Leipzig won against Saarbrucken and rose into the second division. The team has thus been promoted for the third time within the last five years in front of scenery of 42.700 spectators.[22]

The impressive point in regard to the project of Red Bull is not the success in sport. It is astonishing how many fans are attracted already after five years. How is it possible that the club is able to create interest in that dimension?

1.2 PROBLEM STATEMENT

The present state of research regarding the central core topics shall be considered now. Therefore sport sponsoring, brand management and team identification are shown up roughly to declare the problem statement.

From the traditional perspective sport sponsoring is seen as a typical communication instrument for companies to promote their own products and in consequence to improve the ROI on a long term basis. In addition sport sponsoring was and still is a very popular promotion instrument. The unconscious costumer approach in a comfortable and emotional surrounding offers many advantages over classic advertising. Similar to the changing business competition also communication channels have changed. Anyway the importance of sport sponsoring is still important and become even stronger. But its right sponsoring activities have changed from an independent granting of financial means for product promotion to cooperating and co-creating of the value sport in order to improve brand awareness and brand image. Therefore brand management becomes important on both sides the companies and the clubs or athletes as the case might be.[23]

---

[21] cf. Aleythe, 2013
[22] cf. Machowecz, 2014
[23] cf. Woratschek et al, 2014, p.108-111

In regard of co-operation with clubs the topic "Sponsor fit" is gaining in importance. It describes the necessity that Sponsor and Sponsee match. The more similar the brand-images of both partners are the higher the benefits are for both. From the perspective of the club concerning the sponsor the relevant variables here are seriousness, product-fit, ensuring of autonomy, regional identity, benefits, exclusivity and sports focus.[24]

Considering brand management the current scientific knowledge is an integrated inside-out approach. By implementing brand identity beside of brand image into the concept it will be differed between the management concept and the market perception concept. The brand owner declares the origin, competences, vision values, personality and personality of the brand in order to be perceived as those. The recognized image of the external target group is a symbolic construction within the minds of the stakeholders. Here the brand image is time lagged and may be different which in consequence could require an adaptation. Therefore this way of brand positioning is called "identity-based brand management".[25]

On this subject for professional team sport the Team Association Model (TAM) describes branch specific the brand management of the brand image. The brand image consists out of brand attributes, brand attitudes and brand benefits. The highest relevance for the future behaviour of the customer is the brand benefit. Because a team brand has no specific functional benefit for the customer, the benefits are understood as a bunch of symbol and experiential benefits. Due to that the relevant brand benefits for spectators, fans and supporters of team sport are nostalgia, escape, social interaction, emotions, BIRG, aesthetics, eustress and atmosphere.[26]

Anyway in professional team sport the most important factor from an economic perspective is the success in sport which in turn improves and strengthens the brand image of the club.[27]

---

[24] cf. Woisetschläger et al, 2009, p.5
[25] cf. Burmann & Schade, 2009, p.11-13
[26] cf. Burmann & Schade, 2010, p.6-7
[27] cf. Riedmüller, 2014, p.79

In that context professional clubs have in principle five heterogonous costumer groups. Besides the indirect licensing as explained in chapter 1.1 also direct licensing is profitable. The remaining four groups are firstly agencies, secondly sponsors, thirdly media and fourthly direct and indirect fans as spectators in the stadium and satellite supporters.[28]

The last relevant topic is team identification and is mainly discussed in the north-American sport environment.[29] The most dominant reasons here for feeling identified with the team are family reasons, skills and the appearance of players, friends, geographic items and the success of the team.[30] To sum up the deliberations: the essential link of team identification, brand management and sport sponsoring is identification. Nowadays the companies do not only appreciate customers they need fans.[31]

From the perspective of Red Bull the club RB Leipzig seems to fit perfectly to the sponsor. The co-creating of the value sport promotes in an ideal way the product of Red Bull and improves the awareness and image of the company's brand. Furthermore the identification with the brand becomes more intense and thorough.

But if the team brand RB Leipzig is considered independently, without a connection to the company behind the project, the aspect of autonomy and regional identity become confusing. Many studies and concepts elaborate team identification from the view of established clubs who have a long history and an established brand image in the customers' mind. In the case of new team identification only north-American sports franchise and Australian sports franchise are described in literature so far. In the case of Red Bull maybe the target of the project with Leipzig is to move the identification into the direction of the sponsor.

Precisely because the team brand RB Leipzig got some disorienting characteristics the central research question is: Can an identity based team brand be created through a strong sponsor?

---

[28] cf. Schilhaneck, 2006, p.286
[29] cf. Lock, 2009, p.5
[30] cf. Wann, 1996, p.201
[31] cf. Zimmermann & Naskrent, 2010, p.49

1.3   OUTLINE OF THE STUDY

To answer the research question the upcoming action list will be examined.

A. Introduction – Chapter 1
-    Motivation
-    Problem Statement
-    Outline of the Study

B. Theoretical Framework (secondary Analysis) Chapter 2-4
-    Sport Sponsoring (purpose und benefit)
-    Brand Management (in General and in Team Sport)
-    Fan Behaviour (causes and directions)

C. Research Design (definition of sub questions) Chapter 5
-    Background Analysis of RB Leipzig (origin and intention)
-    Research Approach (intention and expected results)
-    Questionnaire Structure (in connection to literature)
-    Data Collection (online and face to face)

D. Data Analysis and Interpretations (primary analysis) Chapter 6
-    Failure Analysis
-    Empirical Findings
-    Interpretation

E. Conclusion and Implications – Chapter 7
-    Limitations and Future Research
-    General Summary and Derivation
-    Implication for Management

Table 1.1 The study´s line of action

To reach profound information for the central question several fields will be enlightened. In chapter 2 the topic sponsoring in sport gives an overview about the relevant research field. Moreover the first sub question has to be answered: Which benefits do sponsors have from a partnership with sport clubs and which forms of implementation are there?

Following from the previous thoughts chapter 3 intends to explain the relevance of building a strong brand and show up which instruments are necessary for that. Coming from general brand management this segment specifies the development in that field and approaches into the direction of professional team brand management. This in consequence should help to answer the second sub question: Which factors influence the brand image in professional team sport and is it possible to influence those factors? To sharpen that understanding chapter 4 goes further into detail and explains causes and direction for the identification with a club or other objects. Out of that concept the third and last sub question of the secondary analysis will be answered: What are the strongest and most important reasons in identification for a fan with a professional football club?

Chapter 5 consists mainly out of three parts. First the youngest history and the direct surrounding of RB Leipzig will be reflected. Also the intention of the sponsor and aims of the whole project are shown up. Second the collected information of the literature review is projected on the club. By successfully translating and transforming it, the brand personality and the self-concept of RB Leipzig shall be outlined. Third the construction of the survey is described and the expected results are explained. This in sum serves as the basis for the questionnaire which is examined by collecting data man-to-man and online. In chapter 6 the quantitative primary analysis finds his final through illustrating, interpreting and proving the results in terms of technique and content. The final chapter 7 concludes the provided information of the whole work and attempts to answer the central research question. Also the limitation of the research design and implications for the management are discussed.

The major target here is to define the origin of the identification. In other words we shall try to answer the question: is the fan's identification with RB Leipzig based on the team brand or is it based on the sponsor? But the work is also interested in drawing inferences for team brand management of new clubs in established sport leagues. Maybe it is possible to identify conflicts also in the perceived image of the sport fans. It is at this point impossible to tell if this approach works but to receive indices if the concept could be sustainable is intended. In addition to this the work will neither judge the model of RB Leipzig nor will be tried to give a prediction for the club's success in the future. Also economic aspects of East-Germany are not part of the discussion.

2 SPORT SPONSORING

In common sponsorship is defined as "an investment, of cash or in kind, in an activity, in return for access to the exploitable commercial potential associated with that activity".[32] In other words sport sponsoring has been seen as a commercial tool to communicate where the sponsor provides financial means, services or know-how. In return he expects to receive an equivalent in order to generate a value out of it.[33]

While sport-sponsoring in Germany is nowadays a favoured instrument for companies to address potential consumers the relevant beginnings occur in the 70's. For example the football club Eintracht Braunschweig was the first club in 1973 that had a jersey sponsor in Germany. The sponsor was called Jägermeister whose core business is selling alcohol and provided 100.000 DM per year for presenting its logo.[34] Nowadays the sport sponsoring volume in Germany is much higher which results in an estimated amount of 3.0 billion € for the year 2014.[35]

2.1 CONCEPT AND DISTINCTION

The main attraction for companies is basically to unconsciously advertise their products, services or their brands in a smooth and emotional surrounding. This stays in contrast to classic advertising which is the advantage of sport sponsoring at the same time. But while in the beginning the ROI of a specific product has been focused now the raise of awareness and brand image attributes are of interest from the sponsor's perspective.[36]

But regardless which intermediate targets a company is aiming for in the end economic issues counts. Therefore the measureable targets of the sponsor are turnover, contribution margin, market shares and profitable contracts. In this context the predictive factors who encourage those economic targets are the strength of the company's brand, customer loyalty and sympathy. Especially with partners in sport transfer effects to foster the own brand can be achieved but also those partnerships provide limited success.[37]

---

[32] ct. Meenaghan, 1991, p.36
[33] cf. Woratschek et al, 2014, p.108
[34] cf. Woisetschläger et al, 2012, p.10
[35] cf. FASPO, 2012
[36] cf. Woratschek et al, 2014, p.108
[37] cf. Woratschek et al, 2014, p.108-109

Nevertheless people enjoy it to pursue their hobbies in leisure time. To address potential customers in such an environment offers greater opportunities. For example in a sport or cultural event a sponsor is able to speak directly to a specific target group. In this way a focus on the intended audience is possible to convince them of the positive intentions when supporting the event. This in turn reflects positively on the company's brand image in general. Stimulating consumers regularly in similar contexts enables building confidence with the sponsor in the long term. But this logic shows also that a single advertisement on a banner or a jersey especially as a short time action is not really promising in success. Moreover to communicate a single message might be difficult.[38]

There are several advantages of sport sponsoring in comparison to cultural and socio-environmental sponsoring. For example spectators of tennis, athletics, swimming or horse riding have sport specific attributes and interests. With those huge variety of different forms of sport also different forms of customer groups exist which can be addressed directly. Moreover sport sponsoring as a promotion tool is applicable worldwide. But also the general effect to raise within a relatively short time awareness of the own company makes these tool very attractive. The dynamic and sportive character of sport in general has positive effects both internal and external.[39]

While the positive effects outweigh there are also disadvantages in comparison to the alternatives. Because companies do know of the beneficial effects it becomes more and more difficult to receive an exclusive contract. In addition trough the high demand also the necessary budget raises. But while the awareness can be improved very fast, the effect to improve the own image is much harder to attain, which results in a long lead time until the effects are recognizable.[40]

The consideration in regard to sport sponsoring has been discussed only from the perspective of the sponsor so far. But the counterparts in respective the providers have also changed in the own presentation, communication and management.[41]

---

[38] cf. Woratschek et al, 2014, p.109
[39] cf. Burmann & Blinda, 2004, p.27-28
[40] cf. Burmann & Blinda, 2004, p.28
[41] cf. Woratschek et al, 2014, p.110

The major change is still in progress and describes the shift from a "Goods-Dominant Logic" (GDL) into a "Service-Dominant Logic" (SDL).[42] This is again a reaction to the changing consuming behaviour in the society. The increasing digitalisation leads to a better networking which offers also new consuming possibilities to the terminal devices. Thus potential consumers are not dependent of time and place anymore. Further the density of receivable information leads to an "information overload". Also the opportunities to publish needs, critics and opinions easily in their networks changes passive customers in an increasing number into active ones. This in consequence pushes all forms of media to fight for attention. This again sensitizes the consumer to consider news and messages more sceptical.[43]

In the sport context the consumer is nowadays understood as a prosumer. This word consist out of the words consume and produce and was firstly mentioned by Toffler Alvin. This term was explained in the correlation of the It-world and explains that the well informed and active consumer is also involved in the production process. An attendee of an event is jointly responsible for the creation of the atmosphere and consumes the outcome at the same time. Therefore in the understanding of SDL value will always be co-created and a differentiation between goods and products is not possible anymore.[44] This means all economies are service that aim at a relational exchange with customers and partners. Moreover enterprises are not able to provide a value; they are only able to make a value proposition.[45]

Out of that logic a sport event with all actors like sportsman, spectators, media, agencies, clubs, federations, state, communities and the public are all participators of the value chain. This includes also that every time segment of the event has to be considered. For example every advertisement before the event starts but also post-reporting are important sections of the performance generation. The paradigm shift in sport sponsoring influences also the management of brands of all parties. The building of brand alliances can therefore have advantages against other parties.[46]

---

[42] cf. Vargo & Lusch, 2014, p.4
[43] cf. Woratschek et al, 2014, p.110
[44] cf. Woratschek et al. 2014, p.111
[45] cf. Vargo & Lusch, 2014, p.10-11
[46] Cf. Woratschek et al, 2014, 112-113

The most well-known forms of Brand Alliances in Sport are Naming Rights and Co-Branding. Therefore the marketing with names is a popular method to show a connection between supporter and the sponsored object. For instance stadiums, jerseys, league-names, event or a stint of a race are used for communication. In case of a combined use like stadium, jersey and the ticket at once the sponsoring effect can be multiplied.[47]

The other popular form of marketing in sport is Co-Branding which gains in importance. Mostly two brands building an alliance on a horizontal level in order to create synergy effects. A popular example has been the Co-Branding of the Nike-iPod-Sports kit. A chip embedded in a running shoe which can be evaluated with the iPod after jogging. This in consequence enables completely new possibilities like organizing a virtual event.[48]

Such brand alliances offers several chances which can lead to a win-win situation for both. Beside of a positive image transfer also a raise in attention and brand awareness can be achieved. Further in this way a greater range of associations and a confidence bonus is possible. But Co-Branding can also have negative effects. In case of a complete contrary brand image consumers will be confused. The diffuse brand image would cause a loss of the brand identity in the first and due to a loss of the core client in the second.[49]

Brand management in sport can be differed mainly into two groups. On the one hand there are manufacturers, producers, services, cities and state who operating with sport. On the other hand there are leagues, clubs, federations and events that managing their brand for sport.[50]

In this correlation the delimitation of brand management with sport will be examined at this point. This also means that in the following sections the beneficial of co-branding with an individual sports man, with a sports team and an event will be discussed.

---

[47] cf. Woratschek et al, 2014, p.113-114
[48] cf. Woratschek et al, 2014, p.115
[49] cf. Woratschek et al, 2014, p.116
[50] cf. Woratschek et al, 2014, p.117

2.2 TESTIMONIALS

The advertising with a prominent person, also known as testimonial, is derived from the Latin term "testimonium" and means certificate or proof. In other words the celebrity attests the quality of the advertised product or service. Although the understanding is not uniform in literature, in the following the term will be assumed as the protagonist of advertising. In this context in the Anglo-American sphere testimonials are also known as Endorsee or Celebrity Endorsement.[51]

In the early 90´s only 2.8% of all television advertising has been made with celebrities. Nowadays every 7th commercial is communicated with a prominent. The use of a sport personality is most favoured.[52] This fact is also revealed in a study by Nufer & Rennhak. They have shown that fame differs in its advertising effect on products and brands depending on the celebrity's field of performance. Therefore the perceived credibility and sympathy is the highest for celebrities from the sport sector. In this evaluation actresses are voted in second, followed by singers and politicians. Likewise also active sportsman and woman are higher rated than retired athletes.[53]

Besides prominent people companies also tend to develop their own characters in TV advertising. For example chief of laboratory Dr Adolf Klenk insures regularly the effect of a hair-restorer. Another example is the plumber from Leimen Dieter Bürgy who explains how pitting corrosion can be prevented with a specific detergent. The final example is the staff of a well-known DIY chain who always promises the huge variety of products on the one hand and the great service on the other hand when visiting. All of those mentioned real-life-testimonials have in common that they try to be authentic. However studies have shown that prominent testimonials are in comparison to real-life-testimonials more efficient in both awareness and recognition.[54]

Furthermore, the issues that are targeted with a sports person are similar to the targets of sport-sponsoring. (See figure 2.1) Therefore beside of improving image and awareness, companies are also interested in fostering customer loyalty and maintaining contact with customers. Out of that reasons it is necessary to choose the appropriate testimonial who

---

[51] cf. Nufer & Rennhak, 2012, p.5
[52] cf. Kilian, 2014, p.196
[53] cf. Nufer & Rennhak, 2012, p.18
[54] cf. Kilian, 2014, p.197-198

fits best to the relevant target group. The use of the sportsman is therefore dependent on success in sport and also the type of sport.[55]

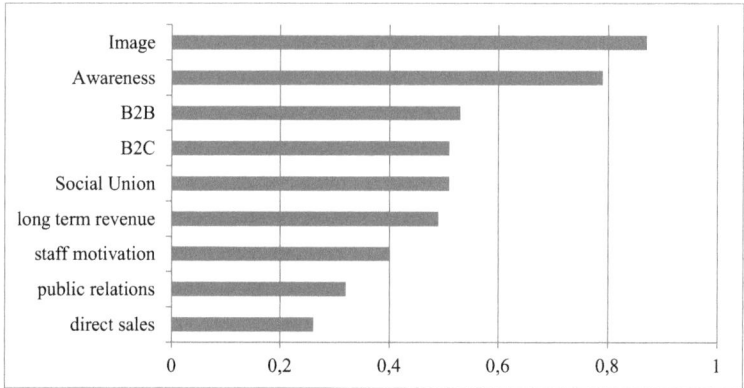

Figure 2.1 Targets of Sport sponsoring[56], own illustration

The process of implementing a testimonial properly has to be carefully aligned. In this correlation the success factor is in consequence the image and awareness in general and the fit with the relevant brand and product in regard to the target group. In literature a three-step process is suggested. In the first phase all relevant attributes that will guarantee an advertising success will be identified. Second a testimonial is selected logically who matches best with the elaborated attributes. In the final phase the attribute overlaps will be highlighted and communicated to the target group.[57]

For this reason several tools to adequately analyse prominent people have been developed. The most established tools in Germany are the "Promi-Check", the "PromiMeter" and the "Celebrity Performance". All tools have in common to target the similarities between personality structure of the brand and the testimonial. The Promi-Check is taking the perspective of the costumer and determines the attitude in several life situations, hobbies and media usage. In the sum 210 questions will be asked to investigate which of each causes a positive or a negative feeling. This results in a condensed psychological profile of the target group where important values will be highlighted. This tool is normally used to create a basis for setting up a proper strategy

---

[55] cf. Kilian, 2014, p.195-197
[56] cf. FASPO, 2012
[57] cf. Kilian, 2014, p.201

14

for brand management but it can be also used to identify a proper testimonial. Nevertheless the prominent is finally chosen in connection to sympathy and awareness within the target group.[58]

In the PromiMeter 1.000 representative people were asked with photographic images. Those people have to judge how each of 8 selected celebrities are perceived in regard to sympathy, awareness, personality structure and the branch specific fit. In this way more than 1.000 celebrities have been evaluated since 1995. In a similar way the Celebrity Performance Index (CPI) evaluates the strength of the image and awareness of the prominent. The factors who define the strength are popularity, credibility, trustworthy, leaders of opinion, positive perception, uniqueness and expectations for success. [59]

In considering the strength of image as one axis and the awareness as another axis a four-field matrix can be sketched. These results in six different performer types because the field at the top right is again further divided in dependence of the intensity. (See figure 2.2) The good, high or ultra-high performer has a high degree of familiarity and a strong image which makes him useable nearly everywhere. A prominent that has both a low strength in image and a low awareness is called low performer and is useable only at niche markets. Further for example a golf-professional who has a strong image but lacks in awareness is named targeted performer and may address interesting target groups. In the last field especially campaigns who want to attract attention a prominent with a strong image and high awareness called attention performer will be useful. [60]

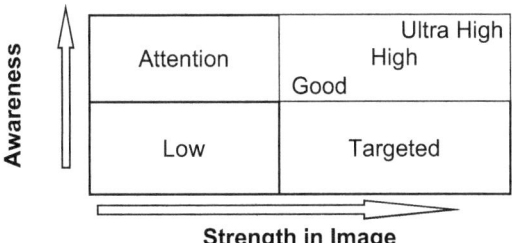

Strength in Image

Figure 2.2 Types of Performers[61], own illustration

---

[58] cf. Kilian, 2014, p.203
[59] cf. Kilian, 2014, p.204
[60] cf. Kilian, 2014, p.205
[61] cf. Kilian, 2014, p.206

2.3   SPONSORFIT

In the context of Co-Branding especially the sponsoring of sport teams respectively football clubs foster the highest interest of every branch in Germany.[62] Especially the regular reporting in all forms of media and the high audience response shows that football is the most popular sport in Germany. The high degree of awareness attracts many partners of the industry and service sectors. But similar to testimonials if not even more the fit between sponsor and club is highly important.[63]

Since 2008 the research group around Woisetschläger has investigated on an annual basis the brand transfer effects of German football clubs and their sponsors. In the beginning they localized the most important factors that make a partnership successful. They found out that sponsor and sponsored party have matched together which again can be positively influenced trough seven determinants. From the perspective of the target group these determinant are sincerity, product fit, regional identity, benefits, exclusivity, sport-relation and maintaining autonomy.[64] (See figure 2.3)

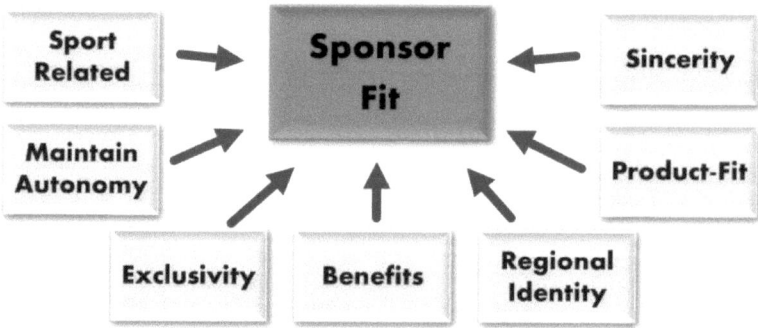

Figure 2.3 Determinants of Sponsor fit[65], own illustration

The fans are reacting displeased when a sponsor attempts to influence the operating business of the club. A sponsor who is not highlighting his interests that much will be positively evaluated by the fans. Because fans also make a cost benefit comparison regarding the sponsor which cannot be calculated out in numbers the perceived benefit

---

[62] cf. FASPO, 2012
[63] cf. Woisetschläger et al, 2012, p.7-10
[64] cf. Woisetschläger et al, 2009, p.11
[65] cf. Woisetschläger et al, 2009, p.3

16

will be judged. Another issue is a sincere and interested behaviour concerning the club and this partnership. Fans are interested in sponsors who strive together with the club for higher goals. If fans feel that the interest of the sponsor lays in profit maximisation the sponsor fit is reducing. A diversified sponsor who is sponsoring too many parties will be realized as unauthentic and can in turn have negative effects toward his image. The general relation to sport or football is an advantage for the sponsor fit exemplified by manufactures of sport equipment. The closeness to the target group appears as suitable for all participated parties. If the origin of the sponsor is similar to the origin of the club, the sponsor fit will rise, because fans perceive this connection as appropriate and useful. Finally a sponsor who shows interest in supporting sport in general fosters the sponsor fit. [66]

Before we illustrate current results of Co-Branding effects of clubs from the German Bundesliga we demonstrate how important the success especially in team sport is. The intertwined relation of success in sport, brand-management and economic success leads to a circled cause-and-effect situation which is explainable as follows.[67]

A club who is able to formulate realistic and clear targets will build up trust with fans if those targets are also achieved. By underlining the typical and unique character of the own club the brand image can be improved and strengthened. In the long run a strong bond will occur and the potential that those fans recommend their supported club is rising. Such a fostered bond enables also to demand premium prices for tickets and merchandising products. The represented brand attract also partners from the industry because the stable, exclusive and distinctive character of the club is positive predictable. The growing offers of potential partners in industry and commerce enables to choose not only out of monetary issues. Therefore the exchange of values can also be examined in form of personal, know-how and strategic issues. In consequence of the clear alignment premium prices price can be demanded also from the partners. The improved financial situation offers the opportunity to buy better players, coaches and sport related facilities which again makes it easier to achieve the formulated targets. These explanations illustrates also how important it is to clearly align the club.[68]

---

[66] cf. Woisetschläger, 2009, p.11-12
[67] cf. Riedmüller, 2014, p.76-77
[68] cf. Riedmüller, 2014, p.78-79

As already stated the sponsor partnerships of the German football clubs have been investigated since several year. To measure the annual changes the relevant clubs and sponsors are evaluated in regard to the perceived awareness and attitude. The data evaluation is performed by an online survey. Similar to the CPI the variables awareness and attitude respectively responsibility is sketched on a four-field matrix which results in four types of Co-Branders (See Figure 2.4). In this way 68 Co-Branding partnerships have been evaluated in 2014.[69]

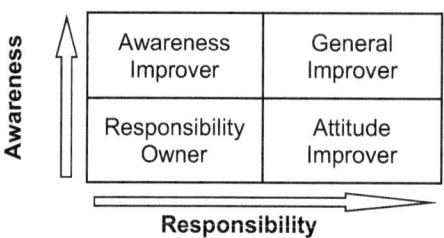

Figure 2.4 Types of Co-Branders[70], own illustration

In the bottom left square mainly sponsors are identified who have an established brand and showing an evolved partnership over a long time like Audi and VW. The same regional and historical background observable on the hand at Audi and Ingolstadt and on the other hand VW and Wolfsburg makes them to responsibility owners. Further examples are TUI and Hannover, Henkel and Dusseldorf or Grundig and Nuremberg. In the next square bonds are identified whose partnership improved the sponsor's awareness in the society. The awareness improvers are mainly used of foreign companies to push their own brands. For example the connection LG Electronics and Leverkusen or Emirates and Hamburg are typical for those type. The category attitude improver is attractive for companies who are already known but who are interested in enhancing their brand image. Likewise successful clubs like Dortmund with their partner Opel and Monchengladbach with Postbank show up these kind of connection. In the remaining square in which attitude and awareness will be improved are called general improver. These type is in regard to sponsor fit and jointly communication effectively for both parties. Especially the most successful teams in the previous season serve those characteristics. A typical example here is the partnership of Munich with their partners Telekom, Allianz and Hypovereinsbank.[71]

---

[69] cf. Woisetschläger et al, 2014, p.6
[70] cf. Woisetschläger et al, 2014, p.10
[71] cf. Woisetschläger et al, 2014, p.9

2.4 EVENT MARKETING

After discussing the potential benefits of Co-Branding with a single person and a team finally the purpose and benefits of event marketing shall be examined. In contrast to the previous explanations, the success in sport of the sportsman and woman of an event like the Olympian Games or the FIFA world cup, plays a secondary role.[72] This is explainable with the significant co-creation character of an event. Due to this logic the protagonists of an event are the spectators and of course consumers at the same time. The spectator reacts on the given proposal of the organizer and judging already during the consumption process. The potentially produced atmosphere in the stadium is again communicated to other parties.[73]

Out of that understanding event marketing is typically experience oriented, interactive, staged and internally initiated. Moreover the event as such is therefore understood as an instrument to communicate with specific audiences. Nevertheless organizers of events can be divided into two groups which are private or public events. But while the private events are normally organized for fostering the own brand or promoting a specific product [74] public events a driven by more abstract and diverse goals. Organisers of such public events would cities and countries which have in the end still monetary issues in mind. Successfully organized events –though they might be expensive- entail financially beneficial effects, e.g. media attendance or attracting tourists on the one hand and improve their citizens` quality of life on the other hand in regard of the city. Especially these objectives are realizable more easily with sport-events because these type attracts the broadest audience.[75]

Out of that reason organizers understand more and more that it is useful to communicate the soul and the character of the city uniformly to create a clear picture over time. Therefore brand management also in regard to cities is becoming more important. For example the pyramids are associated with Egyptians, the Great Wall are associated with China and Paris comes in mind when the Eiffel tower is mentioned. While those regions and cities might not have intended to establish a brand, nevertheless they are able to highlight these attributes and use them as widely recognised logo. Further associations

---

[72] cf. Linley, 2014, p.249
[73] cf. Woratschek, 2014, p.112
[74] cf. Nufer & Scheurecker, 2008, p.4-6
[75] cf. Linley, 2014, p.235

who deals with the location and sport are for example the Olympic Games and Greece or the Circus Maximus and Rome.[76]

The task for cities is therefore to build up other features who are typically associated with them. Each city has its own character and is perceived differently from external and internal people. Nevertheless studies have shown that many cities propose to be dynamic, healthy and progressive. However the perceived character is different and cities can be therefore arranged in three categories. A leading city is for example London and New York while Milan, Wellington and Melbourne are perceived as stylish cities. The cities Vancouver, Copenhagen and San Francisco are perceived as being friendly. As an event venue these individual characteristics can be highlighted and be strengthened.[77]

A study of Brand Capital in 2009 investigated how events influence the location. They proofed that sport and cultural events can influence the character of a city. Further also found out that sport events are associated with dynamic and progressive features and cultural events are associated with stylish, fun and social features. Moreover people who associate a specific city as a location which organizes many events, evaluate the city also as an attractive place to live or to work.[78]

In consideration of the given examples one conclusion can be drawn. A league offers all opportunities for sponsors. First through the huge variety of players who plays in several club a wide choice is provided to use an appropriate one as a testimonial. Second to use of alternating clubs for one specific message offers the possibility to communicate with a huge range of different target groups. These could be possible through Co-Branding with the League Association which in consequence gives the message more credibility. Finally the regular stage of events on a weekly basis improve the image of the several cities on the one hand and improves the awareness of the sponsor on the other hand. The multiplied advertising effect through communication at several places at the same time is a noticeable fact to take a partnership with a League association into account.

---

[76] cf. Linley, 2014, p.237-238
[77] cf. Linley, 2014, p.240-241
[78] cf. Linley, 2014, p.248-249

3 TEAM BRAND

In the world of sport commercialisation and professionalization are increasing. Consequently the importance of a strong brand becomes significant from the economic perspective. Especially in professional team sport it is possible to decouple the success in sport from the relevant target group through an improved brand management.[79]

But the awareness of the three specifics in team sport which includes high consumer diversity, problems with marking of the offered service and speciality of the production process has to be understood. First to manage the various needs and requirements of the five costumer group's media, direct and indirect spectators, sponsors, agencies and licensee has to be clear and consistent. Second the produced service cannot be marked directly which leads to the consequence of alternative marking. Therefore substitute objects have to be found like stadium, training grounds, tickets, dress codes for employees, boards, club rooms or flags marked with the own logo or colour. Third and maybe the most relevant characteristic lies in the creation of the service. Especially team brands who promise constant quality have to consider the dependency on the opponents' performance. To call it competitions there have to be at least two parties. Because the competition is produced together it's also "Co-production". But clubs can solve this problem of varying quality through guaranteeing a thrilling and diversified framework programme inside and outside the stadium.[80]

Regarding team brand management the current state of academic research evolved through the adaption of the conceptual framework on brand equity of Keller (1993) into the team association model by Gladden and Funk (2002) and embedding it into the theory of identity based brand management by Burmann and Meffert (1996) in adding brand identity into the concept especially for team sport (2009).[81]

---

[79] cf. Burmann & Schade., 2009, p.10
[80] cf. Schilhaneck, 2006, p.286-287
[81] cf. Burmann & Schade., 2010, p.4

3.1   TYPES OF BRANDS

In comparison with another brand customers are willing to pay a price premium which is also an indicator of loyalty.[82]These definition stands in correlation to the effectiveness of a brand. But the understanding of the term brand has changed over the last 50 years.[83] But first of all is not tried now to give a complete overview about this topic, nevertheless a rough sketch will be given.

Therefore in the beginning years respectively in the 60´s the feature-oriented understanding has dominated in regard of a brand. This approach occurred through the idea to create differentiation against other providers. Later the sight on the product has changed and the sight from the perspective of the consumer came up. Out of that several groups in the early 70´s started to discuss which factors of the brand have an effect by the customers. [84]

Moreover in the 90´s also in order to determine the brand equity groups started to determine sub-terms of the generic term brand.[85] At this time also an integrated approach has been discussed. In other words both perspective of the provider and the costumers were combined in one approach.[86] These decade also gave brands an own personality on the one side and emphasizes that brand can exist also in any other possible ways on the other side. Nowadays the brand is driven by communication in general and in communication style with customers in order to create a durable connection with them.[87]

Summing up the understanding of the term brand changed with the perspective, the extension of the conceptual framework and the techniques to reach potential customers. This is one major reason for the huge variety of different categorizations in regard to the term brand. [88]

Because brands exists at all branches, also in the sport surroundings the term is highly discussed. Therefore several meanings and types of brand who have a sport context are shown in the following. To provide facts how a brand has to be essential elements and functions of the brand for the provider and the customers are given.

---

[82] ct. Aaker, 1996, p.106
[83] cf. Kaiser & Müller, 2014, p.30
[84] cf. Kaiser & Müller, 2014, p.31
[85] cf. Keller 1993, p.1
[86] cf. Burmann & Meffert, 1996, p.35
[87] cf. Kaiser & Müller, 2014, p.30-31
[88] cf. Kaiser & Müller, 2014, p.30

First of all a brand must have some essential elements in order to be realized as one. For this reason a brand has to have an indistinguishable characteristic to be differentiable against others. However a brand can exist as nearly everything what might be possible. Therefore a symbol, person, service, also an organization or a league is imaginable but also just a letter, a number or a colour are possible to exist as a brand. The pre-condition is that people have an awareness of the brand-exist because only after they can create an association and an image of the brand. To secure a durable success it is necessary to have both a clear message and a continuous improvement to stay in mind.[89]

As a consumer a brand has first and foremost a function for them. In everybody's mind there is a distinctive and unique imagination of the brand. By buying, using and showing the affiliation with the brand the consumers is also trying to differentiate from others. Therefore the consumer expects a constant type and quality of the preferred brand. If these facts are guaranteed he might be able to identify with the brand to receive for example prestige and confidence. The brand has also the advantage to provide a faster orientation in buying decision which discharges them from regular evaluation. Not only but especially in the sport context to express the affiliation with a player or a team is an emphasizing of the own personality. [90]

From the perspective of the brand owner the functions of the brand are different. One of the first functions ever has been the protection of the own brand. But also in case of diversification of the product range the provider can mark his new products and services with his advantageous sign. If the brand is unique the distinguishing itself from other competitors is easier. The creation of preferences helps both to stay in a competitive market and to demand a price premium. The brand of the owner's perspective secures also costumer relations and provides also transfer functions with potential partner.[91]

Because so far the varieties of brands are explainable trough the historic relevance and functions for each, the term is also characterized that people tend to give them a personality. In a study especially designed for football teams in Germany the characteristics and typical features have been determined to measure the personality of

---

[89] cf. Preuss, 2014, p.9-10
[90] cf. Preuss, 2014, p.12-15
[91] cf. Preuss, 2014, p.13-17

each club. In addition the study has been examined online in 2007 by Alexa with a sample size of 8400. The target of this approach has been to give the clubs a tool to compare actual versus target personality of their brand. Through interviews with experts first and a survey with football fans second 24 typical features were found and clustered in four categories.[92] (See figure 3.1)

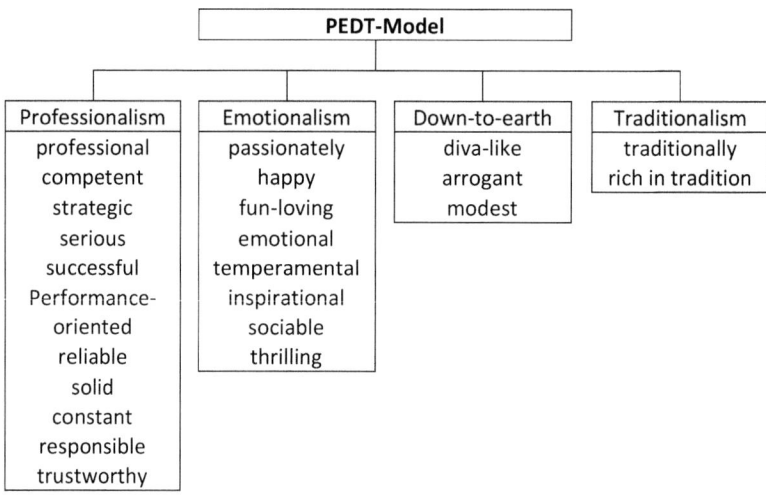

Figure 3.1 PEDT model[93], own illustration

The main categories are professionalism, emotional, tradition and down to earth. As typical representatives of the group professionalism teams like Leverkusen and Bayern Munich were determined. In the group of emotionalism teams like St. Pauli and Cologne are mentioned as typical. The clubs Karlsruhe and Rostock are seen as teams who are Down-to-earth. Finally fans identify clubs like Kaiserslautern and Monchengladbach as typical traditional.[94]

The evaluation of Alexa was a first step to allocate the clubs features and characteristics. To sort these clubs into different types of brands Bühler and Scheuermann examined a study in 2011 to research the opinion of 5400 handball, football and basketball fans in Germany.[95]

---

[92] cf. Alexa, 2014, p.174-177
[93] cf. Alexa, 2014, p.178
[94] cf. Alexa, 2014, p.179
[95] cf. Bühler & Scheuermann, 2014, p.130

In considering which types of brands exists in German professional sport, five different types were determined. The various categories are defined by its brand attributes:

The Champions brand is characterised by dominance in sport and in economic attributes, they are also defined by extreme polarised acceptance of the fans. Fans feel either a high attachment or an extreme aversion concerning the club. The Tradition brand is specified through numerous achievements and titles in the past, but still now the club got a good name. The club possesses high sympathy also in rivalled fan groups. The Iconic brand is determined by an extraordinary distinctiveness. The supporters are highly identified with the club and own a huge fan base. They receive also high acknowledgement by competing supporters. The Test-tube brand is described thereby that structures are created artificially in a short time and with a huge invest. Out of that reason there is now evolved tradition. The fan base is typically quite small. The local-regional brand ("local hero") is defined through an extreme incarnated fan group who comes mainly from the own region. But, the club receives no attention outside of this area.[96]

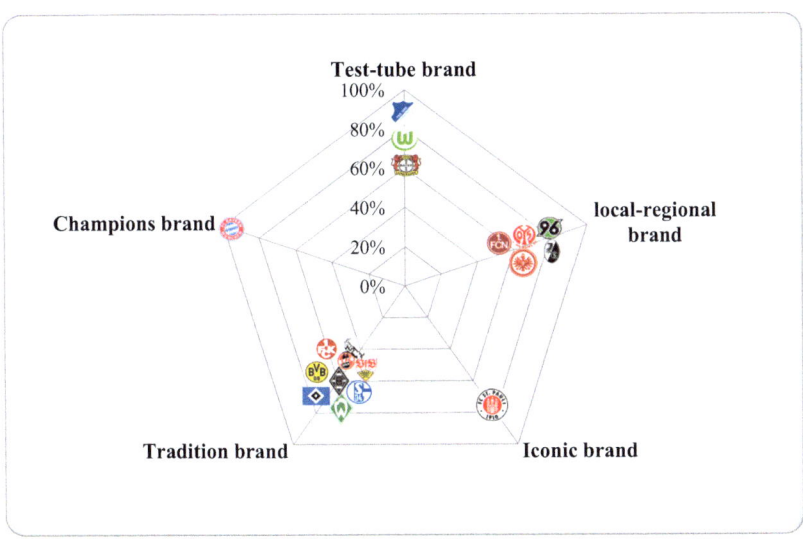

Figure 3.2 Brand Net of the Bundesliga clubs[97], own illustration

---

[96] cf. Bühler & Scheuermann, 2014, p.131
[97] cf. Bühler & Scheuermann, 2011, p.49

In the end all clubs of the first division in the sport football, handball and basketball were sorted in dependence of clearness in a brand net. Caused of its relevance only football clubs were shown in figure 3.2.[98] In addition the sport fans have been also asked if it's important for them that their favourites club is perceived as a true brand. In the sum 58.1% of the sport consumers show that the function of the brand is important for them. While the desire that their club is perceived as a true band is equal for both football and basketball fans with around 52% the basketball fans vote with almost 65%.[99] The football fans have been although asked which club is from their own perspective except of their favourites club a true brand. The result shows that out of 36 professional football clubs only 4 are perceived as true brands. These clubs are St. Pauli, Bayern Munich, Borussia Dortmund and Schalke 04.[100]

However in regard of categorization the club Bayern Munich was elected from the majority of 89.7% of all football fans to be a champions-brand. As the most typical iconic brand fans have voted with 76.2% the club St. Pauli. The representatives of local-regional brand are clubs from Freiburg and Hannover. In the category tradition are the most clubs from Bundesliga like Schalke and Dortmund. In regard to Schalke it was observable that the club are perceived as both traditions-brand (49.8%) and as iconic brand (26%). Typically for a test-tube brand is the club Hoffenheim with 93.3%. [101]

3.2   GENERAL BRAND MANAGEMENT

From an academic perspective the topic brand management is strongly characterised by David A. Aaker and Kevin Lane Keller's works in the 90´s. Not only because its importance for succeeding researchers also caused by its relevance until today we will discuss Keller's paper "Conceptualizing, Measuring, and Managing Customer-Based Brand Equity". His work was mainly thought to determine the value of a brand for accounting perspectives respectively for strategic reasons. Nevertheless the sketch about the dimensions of brand knowledge was pioneering and will be therefore explained in the following (see figure 3.3).[102]

---

[98] cf. Bühler & Scheuermann, 2014, p.133
[99] cf. Bühler & Scheuermann, 2011, p.13
[100] cf. Bühler & Scheuermann, 2011, p.22
[101] cf. Bühler & Scheuermann, 2014, p.135
[102] cf. Keller, 1993, p.1

„A brand can be defined as a name, term, sign, symbol, or design, or combination of them which is intended to identify the goods and services of one seller or group of sellers and to differentiate them from those of competitors".[103] When consumers think about a brand it is important to understand their logic and structure behind. It is also necessary to understand in which order brand knowledge is working. Therefore in the first dimension it will be differed between brand awareness and brand image. Brand Awareness can be understood as the probability consumers think under certain situations about a specific brand.[104]

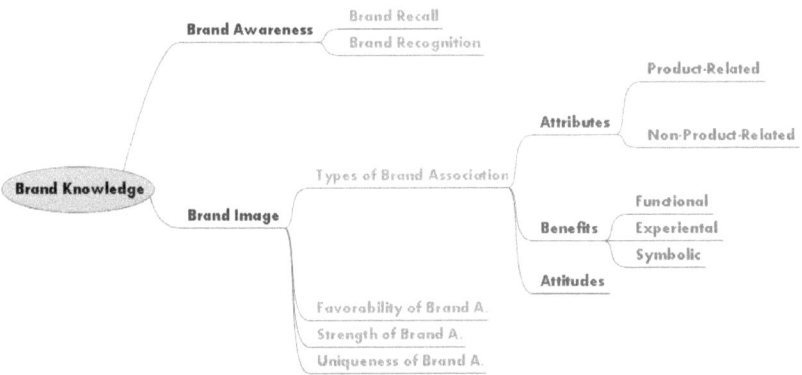

Figure 3.3 Dimensions of brand knowledge[105], own illustration

In this correlation the subsequent dimension of brand awareness is brand recognition and brand recall. Brand recognition in this context means the correct determination of the brand through previous knowledge. This happen for example when the consumer visit a store and recognize the brand correctly when seeing it. In the case of brand recall the consumer is generating the brand from memory. By getting a cue or when the product category is given the consumer thinks about the brand. Brand awareness is already important on a low level. In this way the relevant brand becomes a member of the consideration set of a costumer. Moreover the brand awareness also influences the brand image which is from the perspective of brand knowledge on the same level.[106]

---

[103] ct. Kotler, 1991, p.442; cf. Keller, 1993, p.2
[104] cf. Keller, 1993, p.2-3
[105] cf. Keller, 1993, p.7
[106] cf. Keller, 1993, p.2-3

The brand image corresponds with the meaning of the brand from a consumer perspective. Therefore the favourability, uniqueness, strength and types of association with the brand define the brand image. The strength of the association's correlates both with the quantity and the quality of information that comes in mind when consumers thinking about the brand. In other words the strength is both the amount of data that are connected with the brand and the level of depth in processing this data. When the brand recognition and recall rising to a specific point consumer starting to believe that the brand has attributes and benefits who satisfy their needs. At this point consumer evaluate this brand as favourable in comparison to others. But this favourability of associations occurs only if those products and services are already important for the consumers. In case of an incomparable association which with the brand a unique selling position can be proposed at the market. This is called uniqueness of brand associations.[107]

All forms and information that are associated with a brand are subsumed in the types of brand associations. Those types can be categorized into attributes, benefits and attitudes. Further the sub-dimension attributes and benefits are again subdivided and require explanation. The brand attitude is on the one hand the salient belief a consumer has about the brand and on the other hand the evaluative judgment of that belief.[108]

The brand attributes are differed in product-related and non-product-related attributes. Those attributes are allocated in dependence on how direct there are related to the product. In this context the product-related attributes relates to the physical composition of the product or the service´s requirement. The non-product-related attributes are subdivided again into four categorizations who are defined by the external aspects when consumers coming in contact with the product. These four dimensions are price information, packaging or product appearance information, user imagery and usage imagery. While the user imagery describes which person uses the product, the usage imagery describes at which situation and where the product is used.[109]

The remaining sub dimension of brand association is brand benefits. It is defined by all individual values a consumer connects with a product. These values are differed into

---

[107] cf. Keller, 1993, p.3
[108] cf. Keller, 1993, p.3-5
[109] cf. Keller, 1993, p.4

functional, experiential, and symbolic benefits. First the functional benefits are characterized through the intrinsic advantages when the consumption takes place. Those benefits include solving or avoiding a problem and receiving safety and physiological needs. Second the experiential deals with the feeling when consuming the product or the service. Relevant issues are diversity, sensory pleasure and mental stimulations. Third the group of symbolic benefits means the extrinsic advantages at the consumption of the product or the service. This category is targeting on self-esteem aspects like receiving prestige, being fashionable and getting something exclusive.[110]

This illustrated concept explains many terms of brand management and is also relevant for upcoming chapters. Nevertheless to complete the understanding of missing terms the dimensions of brand personality of Aaker, J.L. are roughly discussed. Brand personality is defined as "the set of human characteristics associated with a brand".[111] In her study she differed between five possible types of brand personalities. Therefore these brand personalities are Sincerity, Excitement, Competence, Sophistication, and Ruggedness. The term brand personality fits best to the non-product-related attributes. This framework is applicable at all product categories.[112]

3.3   TEAM ASSOCIATION MANAGEMENT

Gladden and Funk developed in 2002 a theoretical framework of consumer-based brand equity especially for team brand management. In their literature review[113] they determined several dimensions which can be associated with team sport. On the basis of Keller's framework the branch specific determinants were sorted into that scheme (see Figure 3.4). The so called "team association model" TAM takes the relevant brand attributes, attitudes and benefits of professional sport teams into consideration.[114] This significant work will be highlighted now.

---

[110] cf. Keller, 1993, p.5
[111] ct. Aaker, 1997, p.347
[112] cf. Aaker, 1997, p.347-348
[113] cf. Gladden & Funk, 2001, p.67
[114] cf. Gladden & Funk, 2002, p.54

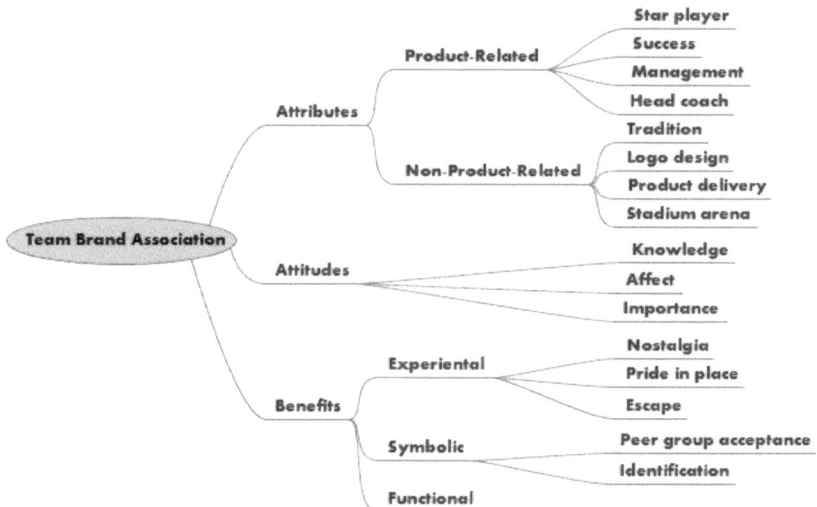

Figure 3.4 Team Association Model[115], own illustration

The first sub-dimension of attributes in this context are product related and represent determinants which supply something to the outcome of the team. This in consequence is a specific star player, an important person from the management, the head coach and last maybe the most important factor success. Especially success pertain the most association with a specific team brand on a long term perspective.[116]

The second sub-dimension of attributes is non-product-related and they are characterized by having no influence on the general performance. Those attributes are logo design, stadium/arena, product delivery and tradition. For example the San Jose Sharks had enormous marketing success just through the Shark logo which was regardless of the success in sport at this time. Which also lead to positive association with the team brand is both positive and negative tradition. For instance the Boston Red Sox are famous through not winning the World Series titles several times in the last century.[117]

The attitudes of brand association for team sport are categorized into three components. First the attitude importance represents the psychological affiliation and value of an individual in regard to a sports team. Second the attitude knowledge describes how much

---

[115] cf. Gladden & Funk, 2002, p.70
[116] cf. Gladden & Funk, 2002, p.57
[117] cf. Gladden & Funk, 2002, p.58-59

an individual knows about this team. Third the affective reactions include all feelings an individual has for the team.[118]

When the product in the team sport context is consumed people receive benefits that satisfy their needs. The functional benefits are discarded because the team sport does not solve consumption related problems. Therefore in TAM the benefits that are associated with a team brand are distinguished in symbolic and experiential benefits. In total five types of benefits are described. In this correlation escape, nostalgia and pride in place are classified into the experiential construct and fan identification and peer group acceptance are classified into symbolic benefits. The element escape describes that sport provides the possibility to escape from daily troubles and routines. Further team sport offers also the connection to the past which is expressed in nostalgia. Pride in place is a beneficial that people receives when consumers have an affiliation with the city. But just the affiliation with the team itself is considered as fan identification. Finally peer group acceptance is the benefit that consumers have when family and friends share their interest in following a team. There is a huge variety in the consuming habit and the people who are consuming team sport. Out of that the classification of the benefits and their borders are not that narrow. In other words in dependence of the individual consumers the benefits for each can be either symbolic or experiential.[119]

Now following is the adaptation and extending of the previous model. This branch specific work has been advanced by Bauer, Stockburger-Sauer and Exler and also poses the current state of research for team brand associations. Basically the adapted model implements the aspects uniqueness, favourability and strength of brand associations in order to improve the causal interrelations.[120] (See figure 3.5)

The first resorting in comparison to the previous model has been made with the item management. Because the management has no influence to the game outcome it was moved from product-related to non-product-related attributes. Further in the previous description the identification was only illustrated for single persons but the awareness of the whole team separately was not considered. In consequence the team and the team

---

[118] cf. Gladden & Funk, 2002, p.61
[119] cf. Gladden & Funk, 2002, p.59-60
[120] cf. Bauer et al, 2008, p.210

performance which includes the style to play are added to the associations of product-related attributes.[121]

Figure 3.5 modified Team Association Model[122], own illustration

Consequently the modifications of the model are also examined in the non-product-related attributes. Here four additional aspects have been found which mainly considers people who indirectly influence the core product. Beside of the attribute management also the attributes the owner or sponsor and fans are part of this association branch. Over a long time all participated people have in addition evolved a specific "club culture and values" who are associated with the club and are therefore also added to these forms of attributes. The fourth and last non-product-related attribute is named regional provenance and describes how the origin influences associations with the team brand.[123]

Moreover Bauer, Stockburger-Sauer and Exler also assumed that attitudes in this context are characterized through an overall judgement of the team brand. Further this judgement is evaluated only on an affective level. Their explanation is based on the typical characteristic of team sport that functional benefits are missing which results in a

---

[121] cf. Bauer et al, 2008, p.210
[122] cf. Bauer et al, 2008, p.211
[123] cf. Bauer et al, 2008, p.211-212

dominated belief system. Fans show on specific level a high commitment to the team and have a strong feeling of attachment to them. Out of those considerations the cognitive elements of attitudinal association's knowledge and importance are rejected.[124]

The final adjustments of the last category are driven by general reconsiderations of both experiential and symbolic benefits. That is why symbolic beneficial is now understood as a fulfilling of internal generated needs like ego enhancement, group membership and role positions. For that reason the item pride in place is resorted because it fits properly to the new formulation of symbolic benefits. In contrast to that experiential benefits are described by cognitive stimulations, emotional enjoyment and sensory experiences. In addition to nostalgia and escape also emotions, entertainment and socializing or companionship are added into the redefined concept therefore. The new aspect socializing respectively companionship reflects the desire of fans to share time and opinions with other unknown but same minded fans.[125]

3.4   IDENTITY BASED TEAM BRAND MANAGEMENT

A significant development in brand management has been made through the extension of the basic model explained in 3.3. While the concept of Keller only illustrates the brand perspective of the consumer the identity based brand management also considers the perspective of the brand owner. This additional perspective offers an improved understanding for brand management in general and provides also strategic elements to align the brand more consequent. In comparison to the traditional branding concept which is an outside-in approach the identity based approach considers both inside-out and outside-in.[126] In general the identity based brand management differs between the self-reflection of the internal stakeholders and the brand awareness of the external stakeholders. (See Figure 3.6)

---

[124] cf. Bauer et al, 2008, p.213
[125] cf. Bauer et al, 2008, p.212
[126] cf. Burmann & Meffert, 1996, p.35

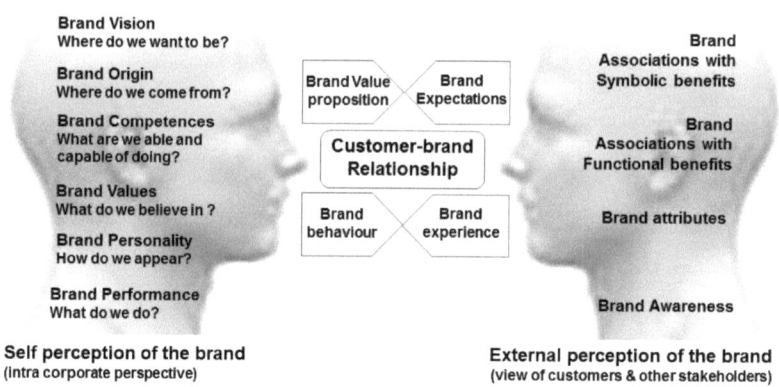

| Management Concept | Market perception concept |
| Brand Identity | Brand Image |

Brand Vision
Where do we want to be?

Brand Origin
Where do we come from?

Brand Competences
What are we able and
capable of doing?

Brand Values
What do we believe in ?

Brand Personality
How do we appear?

Brand Performance
What do we do?

Brand Value proposition — Brand Expectations

Customer-brand Relationship

Brand behaviour — Brand experience

Brand
**Associations with
Symbolic benefits**

Brand
**Associations with
Functional benefits**

Brand attributes

Brand Awareness

Self perception of the brand
(intra corporate perspective)

External perception of the brand
(view of customers & other stakeholders)

Figure 3.6 Principles of the identity based brand management approach[127], own illustration

The researcher Erikson (1957) explains that identity can be evolved either through the individual or through a social group. Brand identity is therefore considered as a form of group identity, which is expressed by a set of commonly shared values, competences, origin, vision, communication style and behaviour.[128] These kind of identity consists out of the relations of the internal group and the interaction with the external group. In consequence the brand possesses a self-reflective identity and are defined as follows: "a spatiotemporal bundle of same oriented features which shapes from an intra-corporate perspective the character of the brand in a sustainable manner."[129] Therefore brand identity can be understood in narrow sense as a concept statement and from a broad sense as management concept.

In the centre of the management concept is the formulation of a brand value proposal for the customers that the brand has to fulfil. This proposal has to be implemented in daily brand behavioural by all brand owners. Out of this deliberations the six components brand vision, brand origin, brand competences, brand values, brand personality and brand performance are derived.[130]

---

[127] cf. Burmann et al, 2003, p.25
[128] cf. Burmann & Schade, 2010, p.3
[129] cf. Burmann et al, 2003, p.16
[130] cf. Burmann & Schade, 2009, p.11

34

In contrast to the brand identity is the brand image a developed mostly time-lagged image of the external target group which evolves over a prolonged period of time. Due to that logic is the external image also understood as the market perception concept. Moreover the brand image is an embedded, compressed and evaluated idea of the brand created by the external stakeholders.[131] The brand value proposition on the one side awakes expectations of the brand on the other side. Those expectations consist out of a bundle of associated benefits of both symbolic and functional nature. Further the functional and symbolic benefits have to be proposed in compressed form to reach a sufficient differentiation in regard to other brands.[132]

A basic antecedent that brand image evolves is the brand awareness. If the brand image is evolved it is composed out of attributes, functional benefits and symbolic benefits. The relevance of buying intentions rises in the following order brand awareness, brand attribute, functional benefits and symbolic benefits. In this correlation the brand attributes represent all perceived properties of a brand from the costumer's perspective. Those properties can be factual, rational, visualized and emotional. Moreover attributes can be also a physical feature or a habit of a typical consumer. However the sum of all brand attributes will be concentrated and judged by the brand consumer.[133]

The brand expectations won't be disappointed if all internal stakeholders behave as the brand values propose, which again guarantees a positive brand experience for the external stakeholders. Therefore all efforts to manage the brand are reflected in the customer brand relationship (CBR). Caused through its economic relevance the CBR is considered as an important key target in brand management.[134]

The secondary analysis by Burmann & Schade discussed in 2009 the perceived image of team-brands. Moreover they also implemented the TAM into the identity-based brand management approach.[135] By doing so they examined several adaptions of the former team brand image concept. A major difference to the previous model have been made through the implementing of brand personality on the one side and by discarding the

---

[131] cf. Burmann & Schade, 2009, p.12
[132] cf. Burmann et al, 2003, p.3
[133] cf. Burmann et al, 2003, p.6-7
[134] cf. Burmann & Schade, 2009, p.13
[135] cf. Burmann & Schade, 2009, p.7

affective attitudes on the other side. Further they identified the type of sport and the sport leagues as a new product-related attribute.[136] Despite of that the new model defines attributes as an accumulation of partial attributes[137] the allocation of sport leagues and type of sport has to be resorted. Bauer & Stockburger-Sauer & Exler argues that product-related attributes are characterized through the involvement of the game outcome.[138] Therefore the new attribute fits more properly to non-product related attributes.

In addition also other adaptations of the brand image approach by Burmann & Schade are worthy of discussion. The components bask in reflected glory, atmosphere, experiencing a star player and experiencing a battling team are added as new benefits. Moreover the former benefit entertainment is replaced by escape, eustress, and aesthetics. Both Pride in place and peer group acceptance are discarded of the list of benefits. The experiential and symbolic benefits are also translated into a bundle of partial benefits.[139] Similar to the order of buying intention the components of the brand image concept are ordered hierarchically in regard of their behavioural relevance. Therefore brand attribute has the lowest relevance, brand personality is in between and brand benefits has the highest relevance for team brand behaviour.[140]

The listed adaptations above of the brand benefits are questionable for the following reasons. First "basking in reflected glory" is an explanation approach by Cialdini which is again derived by the social identity theory.[141] But in the explanations of Burmann & Schade they refer[142] to the hierarchy of needs by Maslow which is restrictedly correct. (See chapter 4.2) Further the benefit peer group acceptance is explained with peer pressure[143] which also differs from the basic concept derived from the SIT (see chapter 4.2). However in devising the concept "Pride in place" Burmann & Schade missed scientific evidence which can be given with the explanations of external group identities by Heere & James.[144]

---

[136] cf. Burmann & Schade, 2009, p.16
[137] cf. Burmann & Schade, 2009, p.19
[138] cf. Bauer et al, 2008, p.210
[139] cf. Burmann & Schade, 2009, p.19-30
[140] cf. Burmann & Schade, 2009, p.35
[141] cf. Cialdini & Richardson, 1980, p.414
[142] cf. Burmann & Schade, 2009, p.21
[143] cf. Burmann & Schade, 2009, p.24
[144] cf. Heere & James, 2007, p.325

Caused by the aforementioned notes the components of the brand image approach by Bauer & Stockburger-Sauer & Exler are still relevant for further considerations. Nevertheless the identity-based management which considers both the inside-out and the outside-in approach is used as the relevant framework here. Therefore the brand alignment process will be now considered more closely. These discussion provide a better understanding for brand management in general on the one hand and uncovers potential failures in brand communication more easily on the other hand.

To create an ideal brand alignment the six mentioned components have to be assessed properly. First the brand owner makes himself clear where the brand comes from to set up the basis for further deliberations. After clarifying where the brand has its origin the brand specific competences are reflected to know what the competitive advantages of the brand is. Guided by the brand vision which also defines where the brand wants to be the remaining components are determined. Therefore it is necessary to understand the brand performance which is reached by reflecting the brand usage. Further all internal stakeholders have to believe in the same values in order to show in which the brand is believe in. Finally the brand personality conveys at which style the given components are communicated.[145]

The differentiation between brand identity and brand image offers also the possibility to better control the brand. Therefore weaknesses in the brand management can be uncovered through a gap analysis. In this correlation four different gaps are analysed and are as follows: The first gap occurs through a difference between set-point identity and ideal brand image caused by a lack of awareness. For example by ignoring customer needs the management may misinterpret brand expectations. The second gap appears if set-point identity and actual-identity differs. An explanation for such a case is when the implementation of the brand vision lacks for instance through weakness in brand performance. The third gap happens when the communication between brand image and brand identity are incorrect. These gap is observable if the awaken expectations are not covered by the brand. The last gap is shown up when perfect image and the real image differs. The reason could be the result of Gap1, 2 or 3 or if the brand benefits from the perspective of the customer are not sufficient.[146]

---

[145] Cf. Burmann et al, 2003, p.17
[146] cf. .Burmann et al, 2003, p.51

4   FAN BEHAVIOUR

There are several terms for people who participate in team sport like fans, spectators, supporters, viewers or just consumers. But regardless of terminology, individuals differ to the degree they identify with their favourite team or player, whereby identification is the degree to which they feel "psychologically connected" to the team or player.[147] Although many other explanations and definitions occur in the relevant literature, we assume this form of explanation.

In reflecting the topics 'supporting' and 'fan behaviour' mainly two key factors are the drivers therefore. The psychological perspective shows enhancing personal esteem can be achieved either by vicarious achievement or by affiliating with groups of one mind to achieve an impression of community. These approaches are similar to the concept of the social identity theory from Tajfel and Turner (1979).[148] With the following theory we also illustrate the conceptual framework for this chapter.

4.1   SOCIAL IDENTITY THEORY

In a rudimentary and experimental group situation random people were divided into two groups. Each person knows about their own membership but have no idea about each other's belonging. There was no interaction and no group history. The surprising result exposes that each group member always favours the in-group instead of the out-group in cases of allocation decisions. The in-group profit was less important than maximizing the difference between in-group and out-group. This kind of experiment was retried very often and the result was significantly similar each time.[149]

Astonished by the results the scholars Tajfel and Turner (1986) finally derived three basic assumptions through their conclusions. First, individuals strive to achieve positive self-assessment or to improve their self-assessment. Second, one part of the self-assessment is the social identity, which is compounded out of several memberships in

---

[147] ct. Wann et al, 2001, p.3
[148] cf. Kerr, 2009, p.43
[149] cf. Wenzel, 1996, p.120

several groups and their evaluation. Third, the evaluation of the memberships results in comparison through other relevant groups.[150]

The central aspect of the social identity theory is that people possess a motive for positive self-appraisal.[151] As mentioned in the second assumption "One part of our self-concept is defined by our belonging to social groups."[152] Moreover the other part of our self-concept is the personal identity. These consist out of personal characteristics or individual features.[153] To make this theory more clear and to show how Tajfel and Turner reached their assumptions the psychological process will be enlightened now. This process includes categorization, comparison and identifying.

Due to limited processing capacities we define categories and schemes to simplify our understanding of the world. We categorize people into groups; moreover we segment, classify and order the social environment to structure social interactions. The social categorization enables us to examine various forms of social actions. As a result of this we categorize ourselves into groups. That means every person belongs to various groups at the same time, but not each group has the same importance.[154] In this context the word salient is often used, which describes that group belonging has to be relevant, important and aware.[155]

The process of social categorization is linked with comparison. Comparing and categorizing is an evaluation process to determine our place in society. We compare ourselves with other persons, salient groups with other groups and members in the groups to each other. This helps to figure out how decent and appropriate our belonging to each group is. For example by comparing characteristics, meanings and other subjective attributes we know to which group we belong to. The theory of social comparison was first described by Festinger in 1954. But, in SIT the comparison is examined only for relevant groups and persons who are similar to belonging groups and to oneself. The

---

[150] cf. Wagner & Zick, 1990, p.319-330
[151] cf. Wagner & Stellmacher, 2004, p.161
[152] ct. Trepte, 2006, p.255
[153] cf. Wagner & Stellmacher, 2004, p.161
[154] cf. Trepte, 2006, p.257-258
[155] cf. Wagner & Stellmacher, 2004, p.162

relevance rises with similarity, so even more similar a person or a group is even more relevant the result of the comparison becomes.[156]

An essential requirement that comparisons with another group becomes relevant is the internalization of the own group. The social identity is described by the knowledge of the memberships to social groups combined with the value and emotional connotation which are connected to those memberships. Furthermore it is based on the more or less but positive comparison between in-group and out-group.[157]

Because the society is in a continuous process of changing, the social identity is also driven by the permanent motivation of progress. Guided by the main target achieving a positive social identity, dimensions are evaluated whereby the in-group falls at the evaluative positive side. In cases of a negative evaluation, the fundamental motivation for self-esteem leads therefore to several strategies. If the inferiority of the in-group is not deniable the scholars suggest the following possibilities.[158]

The members can change into an improved or superior group; this behaviour is also called "individual mobility".[159] It is possible that the access to the new group is blocked for example by physical reasons, group boundaries or sanctions of the group. In such a case the in-group member can change, add and shift the dimensions respectively redefine the values that are associated with the inferior criterion or compare with a different group. Such a strategic behaviour is called "social creativity".[160]

By transforming the introducing assumptions the SIT is defined by following principles. First, individual strive to achieve a positive social identity, which is completely defined by a membership of one group. Second, a positive social identity is based through a beneficial comparison with a relevant out-group. Third, unsatisfied social identity leads in attempting to leave the own group and to reach a positive one or individuals try to improve the own group to sharpen the positive elements.[161]

---

[156] cf. Trepte, 2006, p.258
[157] cf. Trepte, 2006, p.259
[158] cf. Trepte, 2006, p.259
[159] cf. Wagner & Stellmacher, 2004, p.163
[160] cf. Trepte, 2006, p.259
[161] cf. Wagner & Zick, 1990, p.319-330

40

In 1987, the scholar Turner developed the SIT further and proposed the self-categorization theory (SCT). The SIT, SCT and the "theory of social accentuation" are together the social identity approach. To complete the understanding, the accentuation theory implemented by Tajfel in 1957 and 1959 describes that differences between groups (interclass differences) are emphasized and differences between members of one group (intra-class differences) are underestimated. [162] The SCT in contrast to SIT describes the process of self-categorization more precisely which includes the change of interpersonal behaviour to inter-group behaviour.[163] Caused by its relevance we roughly illustrate the central statements of the SCT. The self-categorization theory proposes that the self-concept is a set of available cognitive representations of oneself.

In this context Turner assumes that there are three dimensions. The concept of oneself as a human being is the highest dimension. Attributing to groups which are similar to oneself is defined as the social dimension. The third one is the individual dimension: that deals with the differences and similarities of in-group members.[164] In regard to behaviour the SCT suggests that individual differences and the collective similarities or rather the personal and the social identity can become salient. Nevertheless also combined forms of salience can occur and depends by the situation.[165] Out of those deliberations several phenomena´s are explained through SCT.

For example if the awareness of similarity to group members is highly salient and a conflict comes up, the sympathy of the group members to each other will rise. The group members are also agreeing in opinion more often. Such an effect is gaining in importance with the intensity of the battle. Many group phenomena are explained by this kind of behaviour.[166] Another form is the stereotyping of oneself or of out-group members. Group members whose attributes are seen as stereotypical were perceived as replaceable and identical.

This in consequence happens also for the self-concept. In case of a salient social identification the individual stereotyping himself through a redefinition of the self. The

---

[162] cf. Wagner & Stellmacher, 2004, p.157
[163] cf. Trepte, 2006, p.257
[164] cf. Wagner & Zick, 1990, p.319-330
[165] cf. Trepte, 2006, p.257
[166] cf. Wagner & Stellmacher, 2004, p.163-164

depersonalisation results through changing unique attributes and individual differences to shared associated stereotypes. The group possess an own reality which cannot be broken down to attributes of one individual.[167] The last example here is the prototypical group position. If group members realize that the average opinion of the in-group is very similar to the opinion of the relevant out-group the own position of the whole group will be shifted to clearly distinguish again. Therefore the opinion and attitude depends always on the intergroup context.[168] The social identity theory is a proven and a popular framework which explains why and how fans identify with their team or club.[169]

4.2   ESTABLISHED TEAM IDENTIFICATION

To determine the specific reasons why people attend sport events and which variables influence the satisfaction of the spectators is a highly discussed topic in the literature. In researching professional team sport the core product still is the live sport event. In that relation "The importance of team identification, or the degree to which an individual feels psychologically linked to a team or a player",[170] is the central point of consideration. Only through the understanding of consumer behaviour, attitudes and desire the product can be placed, packaged, priced and promoted ideal.[171]

Two studies with a total of 546 undergraduates tested the cognitive, behavioural and affective reactions among sport spectators in concern of the team. Both studies found out that people who have a high degree of identification are willing to spend more time and money watching the game and believe in special qualities concerning individuals of the own fan base. Furthermore they are more optimistic about future team performance, attributing team success more to their own ego and asserting to have more involvement with the team than low identified people.[172]

By specific research in football and basketball surroundings (which provide the greatest motivation for team identification) five determinants were found out and are mentioned in the following: the influence of parents and family, the influence of same aged people, skills and characters of players, geographic reasons and success of the team. Nevertheless

[167] cf. Wenzel, 1996, p.122
[168] cf. Wagner & Stellmacher, 2004, p.164
[169] cf. Kerr, 2009, p.43
[170] cf. Wann, 2001, p.3
[171] cf. Greenwood et al, 2006, p.254
[172] cf. Wann & Branscombe, 1993, p.201; Greenwood et al, 2006, p.254

the researchers debate if geography or team success is the strongest factor for team identification. Each result in turn depends on the concept, type of sport and place of the research study.[173]

The research team around Cialdini investigated in three field experiments the reaction of college students after games of their university's American football team. They found out that the students tend to wear school identifying dresses more often if the football team had been won. Moreover the using of the pronoun "we" raised in this interrelationship. Due to their observation they came to the conclusion that people seem to make known a connection to different people who have been successful. This tendency is also called Basking in Reflected Glory (BIRG). Such a phenomenon is less rational but is simply explainable through the awareness of affiliation. It is also explainable if the perceived membership for the individual to that person is relevant. Therefore this appearance is also recognizable in connection to famous people like statesmen, entertainers or beauty contest winners if they grow up or live in same area.[174]

However the target of an individual is to gain esteem therefore displaying the connection to successful people can also be seen as an image-management tactic. Another form of image management in an intergroup context is to damage the image and values of rivalled groups in order to enhance the difference. Such a strategy is called blasting.[175] In understanding the reason a similar behaviour in self-presentation is to decrease one's association with unsuccessful others. This way of self-portrayal is described as Cutting off Reflected Failure (CORF).[176]

In a concept described by Madrigal the implementation of social identity theory and consumer behaviour theory was examined. In his approach he mainly differed between cognitive and affective reasons. Affective parameters are "BIRG" on the one hand and "Enjoyment", described as the pleasure that occurs through consuming the sport event, on the other hand. The three given cognitive factors are quality of the opponent, identification with the team and the match between expectation and happening of the event. The intertwining effect of both factors leads to the subjective impression of

---

[173] cf. Greenwood et al, 2006, p.254-255
[174] cf. Cialdini et al, 1976, p.366-367
[175] cf. Cialdini & Richardson, 1980, p.406
[176] cf. Snyder et al, 1986, p.382

satisfaction. This concept is proved through surveys on spectators of four basketball matches. These studies show up that team-identification influences the factors BIRG and Enjoyment most.[177]

In this correlation the consumer satisfaction theory by Oliver (1993) can explain spectator conative loyalty. The concept of Oliver has some logic sequences that can be applied on spectatorship which are explained below. Purchase and repurchase behaviour of costumers are mainly dependent of quality, satisfaction and loyalty. While quality has a direct influence on satisfaction, satisfaction in turn has a direct influence on loyalty. Out of that a four staged loyalty model is derived.[178]

The lowest level is the cognitive stage in which consumer's behaviour depends mainly on the evaluation of receivable data. The decision at this step is basically driven by the costs of the product or the service. In the next stage the purchase decision is pushed by a combination of experience and feelings. In consequence the affective stage is characterised by liking and disliking the product. When loyalty increases the consumer reaches the conative stage. Here the behaviour is determined by intentions. These can be understood not only for the present action also for the willingness to buy the service or the product in the future. Describing the action stage is the continuing of the explained logic. In the final phase of loyalty alternatives are not considered anymore. Further the purchasing and repurchasing habits are now a routinized response.[179]

Applied for a sports team if the team loyalty is highly developed the identity is strengthened in a way that it is persistent, resistant to change and creates biases in cognitive processing and guides behaviour.[180]

The origin of team identification can also be created through external factors. Mainly demographic categories and membership organizations are identified by this way of connection. This indirect way of identification is derived from the SIT. A sport team that represents a specific group becomes relevant if it is important for the own self-concept.

---

[177] cf. Madrigal, 1995, p.206
[178] cf. Oliver, 1997, p. 418-430, cf. Trail et al, 2005, p.99
[179] cf. Oliver, 1997, p. 418-430, cf. Trail et al, 2005, p.99
[180] cf. Heere & James, 2007, p.331

But while individuals choose to become a part of membership organizations the demographic categories are characterized that members are born into that groups.[181]

To make this clearer several examples are given for each category.

In the demographic category the identity can occur by geographic reasons. These forms of identity are recognizable for cities, states, nationality even for continents.[182] While the New York Yankees are seen for citizens as a symbol of the city's identity, the club FC Bayern Munich represents a whole state in Germany.[183] Especially in inter-country competitions the relevance of national identity is observable. The affiliation with a team which represents a whole continent highlighted through red or blue marking of clothes is noticed at the Ryder Cup where Europe competes against USA.[184]

But beside of geographic reasons the demographic category includes also ethnic, racial, gender-based, sexuality-based and social-class identities. Also for those types several examples can be given.[185] The Spanish soccer club Athletic Bilbao consists only out of Basque players. This in consequence creates affiliation for individuals who belong to the ethnic group Basques.[186] Gender-based identities are observable in north-American basketball. While the audience in the NBA is mainly male the spectators in the female counterpart named WNBA consist in the majority out of woman. Furthermore, the enthusiasm of homosexual spectators at the gay games is also an expression of their sexual identity. The importance demonstrating the attachment to a social class become less important over the last years. But soccer clubs like Schalke and Rotterdam were founded by the workers of nearby fabrics also in order to show their working class identity.[187]

In contrast to the demographic categories the membership organizations are characterized through the voluntary attribution. Typical forms are observable by identities based on vocational, political and religious background. In this context vocational means

---

[181] cf. Heere & James, 2007, p.324
[182] cf. Heere & James, 2007, p.327
[183] cf. Riedmüller, 2014, p.89
[184] cf. Kleffmann, 2014
[185] cf. Heere & James, 2007, p.327
[186] cf. Radler, 2004
[187] cf. Heere & James, 2007, p.328-329

identifying either with the performing profession or the belonging to a specific organization. The similarities to social class identities exists but whereby vocational refers to one specific group or profession a social class consist out of various professions with a broad combination of each. Especially companies in Europe set up Soccer teams in the beginning of the 20th century to strengthen identification and commitment with the firm. Typical examples are the chemical group Bayer and the electronic firm Phillips who founded the clubs Bayer Leverkusen and PSV Eindhoven.[188]

Further political identities are hard to find and overlapping with the issues who were already mentioned. However addressing nationalistic superiority in 1934 the German regime used the Olympic Games as an instrument to express their political identity. A competition between two rivalled football clubs which are symbols for religious belonging is recognizable in Scotland. The catholic club Celtic Glasgow and the protestant club Glasgow Rangers battles annually for the supremacy of the confessions.[189]

The illustrated examples of external factor that creates team identification are from a relatively wide perspective in comparison to the smallest relevant reference group. For example friends, parents, brothers and sisters have a tremendous influence on team identification. In a study by Kolbe and James in 2000 specifically researched the socialization process of sport fans. They found out that roughly three quarters of the supporters of an NFL team become true fans before they reached the 15th birthday. Moreover forty percent named the own father as the main reason for their affiliation.[190]
Share time together with friends or family members when attending games leading indirectly to team identification. But also the involvement possibilities beside of the game can have the same effect. For example fan services, information availability on game schedule, and direct interaction with fans at the homepage, also parking possibilities influencing team identification.[191]

Those mentioned aspects describing features who improve the accessibility to the game. But the sport itself as a higher dimension can also have an influence on the individual

---

[188] cf. Heere & James, 2007, p.329-330
[189] cf. Heere & James, 2007, p.330
[190] cf. Kolbe & James, 2000, p.23-25
[191] cf. Choi et al, 2009, p.270-271

affiliation of the accessible team. Therefore the emotional aspects like escaping from daily business or eustress as the opposite form of stress to stimulate and energize an individual are important factors for individuals. Getting stimulated by just watching the game or through gambling out of economic issues are relent topic for some spectators. In a study the researcher Wann, Schrader and Wilson (1995) found out that people who attend individual and nonaggressive sport have a high interest in aesthetic issues. This stays in contrast to people who attend team sport and aggressive games in order to eustress and to receive self-esteem.[192]

In a study by Jones (1998) especially the fans of a less successful team was investigated. The English club called Luton Town was playing in the Football League Second Division the third highest league in England. For highly identified fans the style of playing was considered to be more important than winning. Moreover the quality of the facilities and general team success has no influence on their identification with the team. Once the identification had developed it was stable over time. The sense of belonging to a social group and social interaction with the fan community is important. For fans the institution provides a place to social interact with same minded.[193] The fan that is highly identified shows both out-group derogation and in-group favouritism. By stressing the positive aspects of being Luton Town fan they show "voice". On the same level they notably dislike the club Watford. Both behaviours were interpreted as actions to maintain identification.[194]

Because team identification is a highly discussed topic the access to that field is simplified by sorting the various motives and causes in groups. Hereby the categorization is leant on the concept by Sloan who differs between four types. Those categories are named stimulation seeking, entertainment, achievement seeking, and social interaction.[195]

In the above lines we already discussed several aspects that have to be sorted by. The external factors like demographic categories and membership belongings but also socialisation factors caused by friends or family are part of social interaction. Moreover the perceived value, enjoyment and consumption aspects are contents of the group

---

[192] cf. Wann et al, 1999, p.114
[193] cf. Jones, 1998, p.243-246
[194] cf. Jones, 1998, p.260-263
[195] cf. Sloan, 1989; cf. Lock, 2009, p.23

entertainment.[196] The motives of the category involvement deal with active participating. Those may be stimulating issues in order to stress or distress, but also aesthetic issues and emotional reasons like being part of a drama regardless if it have a positive or a negative end can be named. The last and fourth group is widely explained and consists of the elements BIRG, self-esteem, and identification with a specific player or a coach. This group can be summarized by the term achievement seeking. The boarder for each group are often fluid, nevertheless this form of categorization is illustrated in figure 4.1.

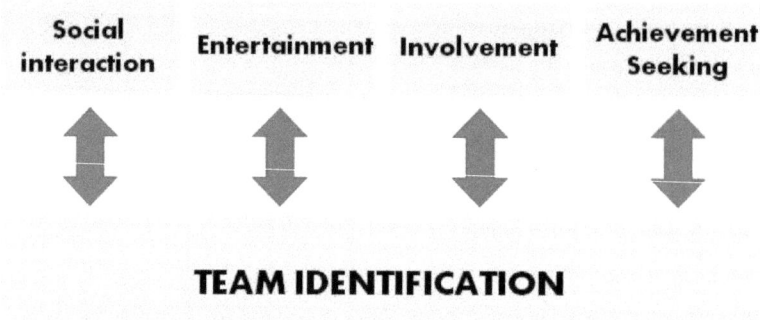

Figure 4.1 Influences and Reasons for Team Identification[197], own illustration

4.3   NEW TEAM IDENTIFICATION

In talking about team identification and to understand the coherences normally clubs with long tradition and history are considered. For these cases the bonds between fans and team have evolved over long time. Regardless of individual participation to a specific point of time the fan community was already existent before. These form also called established team identification has been explained in chapter 4.2. But how is the evolution of identification in the beginning when league and club are newly founded. This topic was researched by Lock (2009) which is in this context described with new team identification.[198]

In a two-season study the researcher Lock followed supporters of Sydney FC a football club in Australia. The specific situation here has been that the A-league examined its first season ever and that the football club Sydney was also founded only three years earlier in

---

[196] cf. Choi et al, 2009, p.270-271
[197] cf. Sloan, 1989; cf. Lock, 2009, p.23
[198] cf. Lock, 2009, p, 166

2004. In the years between 1977 and 2004 a soccer league was already existent. But this league had problems to activate mainstream attendance. The National Soccer League (NSL) consisted out of many clubs who represent several ethnic groups which attract no attention in the broad population of Australia. Due to the experiences of the former league the new founded A-League consists now out of one-team-per-city franchises in order to attract all Australians in the country.[199]

Sport Spectator Identity Scale of Sydney FC		
Total (sample size n = 788)		
	Mean	StDev
Interest in Sydney FC	7,17	1,08
Awareness of being a fan of Sydney FC	6,99	1,14
Importance that Sydney FC wins	6,86	1,14
how Friends see oneself	6,75	1,46
Importance to be a fan of Sydney FC	6,70	1,42
visual identification	4,88	2,22
distinction to rivals	4,58	2,50

Table 4.1 Sport Spectator Identity Scale of Sydney FC[200], own illustration

To evaluate the psychological process and to find the motives for attendance of those fans he examined several surveys. He found out with the sport spectator identity scale (see chapter 4.4) that fans of Sydney FC had a strong commitment already after the first season. With a seven-item, eight-point Likert scale where the highest number corresponds with the strongest commitment the result was also proven in numbers. Therefore after season one the psychological commitment showed a mean in average of 6.14. To judge this result the inventors of this tool valued on undergraduate sport spectators a mean in average of 5.61. In the second season (see table 4.1) the commitment even raises to a value of 6.18 which also show that the formation process is ongoing.[201] In addition the degree of commitment depends on the age. Therefore younger fans shown up in comparison to older fans a stronger affiliation to Sydney FC.[202]

Lock discovered while both cognitive and affective factors are very similar on a high level the behavioural components are differing very strong. Therefore fans show

---

[199] cf. Lock, 2009, p. 73-75
[200] cf. Lock, 2009, p. 132
[201] cf. Lock, 2009, p. 131-133
[202] cf. Lock, 2009, p. 136

significant high interest in following the club Sydney FC on a daily basis but to display their affiliation can be raised further. It also notable that the distinction to rivals is the least pronounced component of all.[203]

Therefore some in-depth interview have been examined to investigate the identification process further. The major finding in this type of analysis has been that new team identification is a developing process. Out of these findings five behaviours characterizes this kind of development which are defined as searching, expression, eagerness, names with faces and spruiking. In the beginning level members show a strong interest in team-related news which correlates with that potential fans actually searching therefore. Over time the affiliation of these supporters will be expressed although by displaying this bond. As a further increase of their belonging fans are now more eager to support their team expressed through visiting the games more often. This process is strengthened that fans are now able to sort the faceless and unknown players the right names by. Described as the final level fans are now recommend the club and the team regularly which is also called Spruiking.[204]

The identification process gives an insight how the commitment raises over time. To identify why people support a football team at the very beginning also the motives have been explored. In the case of Sydney FC tradition and locality are missing which anyway changes the starting situation in comparison to established team identification. The main motive in this context is a strong interest in football. This interest was formulated by fans either to support Australian football or just by the affiliation with the sport in general. Lock explained that constant failures in the national team and the previous league NSL sharpened the view of football fans. Therefore Sydney fans are also supporters of the prior goal improving Australian soccer. The second most reason to support Sydney F.C. has been the affiliation with the city. Regardless of the brief history the origin plays a big role in the identification process. While just the possibility to get entertained at home games is a strong motive for fans to come success is not.[205]

---

[203] cf. Lock, 2009, p.177
[204] cf. Lock, 2009, p.187
[205] cf. Lock, 2009, p.167-170

4.4   TOOLS TO MEASURE IDENTITY

The effort to determine the key factors of team identification goes hand in hand with the inventing of appropriate measurement tools. Basically it can be distinguished between two types of measurement methods. These procedures consider either the socio-psychological involvement or the motives of participating in sport events as a spectator or a fan. Therefore several methods of each type will be presented now.

The main target of socio-psychological tools is to dedicate the degree of identification with specific teams. In a first step various consumer groups can be determined. In a second step further specific demand behaviour and frequency of attendance for each group can be derived. But such instruments are also useful to monitor evolvements and awareness of the bonds with the fans and the team.[206]

1.	How important is it to you that XXX wins?
2.	How strongly do you see yourself as a fan of XXX?
3.	How strongly do your friends see you as a fan of XXX?
4.	During the season, how closely do you follow XXX through the television, radio newspapers, or contact with other fans?
5.	How important is being a XXX fan to you?
6.	How much do you dislike XXX´s greatest rivals?
7.	How often do you display XXX´s name or insignia at your place of work, where you live, or on your clothing?

Table 4.2 Questions of the Sport Spectator Identity Scale[207], own illustration

The first example here is the Sport Spectator Identity Scale (SSIS) invented by Wann and Branscombe in 1993 and has been created to measure the influence on ticket demand. The SSIS can be applied to determine the strength of the identification with a specific team. The tool consists out of seven questions and eight possibilities to answer illustrated by an eight-point Likert scale which ranges from 1 to 8. The lowest number corresponds with the most negative opinion and the highest number corresponds with the most positive opinion regarding the team. (See table 4.4).[208]

---

[206] cf. Choi et al, 2009, p.268-269
[207] cf. Wann & Branscombe, 1993, p.5
[208] cf. Wann & Branscombe, 1993, p.5

An example for a result of an examined SSIS was given already in the previous discussion about new team identification with Sydney FC. The major advantage of the SSIS is the easiness in application and it is fully adaptability to nearly all types of team sport.

Another example identifying the intensity of identification is given with the tool called Psychological Commitment to team (PCT). It consists out of 14 questions and was especially created for NFL teams in order to classify and to determine fan loyalty. The basic concept is to consider the loyalty of fans as a two-dimensional construct. Therefore four different categories results in examining the tool (See table 4.3).[209]

Psychological Commitment

		Strong	Weak
Behavioural Consistency (Attendance Frequency)	High	High (True) Loyalty	Spurious Loyalty
	Low	Latent Loyalty	Low (Non) Loyalty

Table 4.3 Loyalty Model of fans[210], own illustration

For each segment marketing suggestions are given. The fans with frequent attendance and strong commitment for the team are called high loyalty fan. Marketer should try to reinforce this group with economic or personal incentives to strengthen that segment in order to avoid losing them. Spurious loyalty fans who lacks in commitment may be converted through a rationalization strategy. This could happen through promoting the positive attributes of the team and getting the fans to articulate why they support them. The latent loyalty fans who lacks in attendance may be strengthened through an inducement strategy. By removing significant barriers through economic incentives may help.[211]

---

[209] cf. Mahony et al, 2000, p.16
[210] cf. Mahony et al, 2000, p.17
[211] cf. Mahony et al, 2000, p.22-24

The remaining segment characterized through rare attendance and weak commitment are called low loyalty fan. These are the most challenging segment because regardless of the efforts and the expenses to change their behaviour that may be without any effect. Nevertheless either a rationalization or an inducement strategy could also be helpful here.[212]

In contrast to the psychological applications the remaining measurement tools attempt to locate the motives for attending. Dedicating the reasons why people are interested in or connected with a sport, a club, a team or a player gives major insights of the consumer groups to understand and promote them. Also implications for the management may arise through the results.[213] Mainly all the motives of the upcoming scaling tools can be classified into the four categories social interactions, involvement opportunities, perceived value and fan identification already explained in chapter 4.2.

The first instrument explained here is the Motivation Scale for Sport Consumption (MSSC) by Trail and James. It is already an advanced design because it developed and integrated the existing tools SFMS, MSC, and FAM further into one concept. But before explaining the MSSC the three antecedent instruments are roughly sketched.[214]

The Sport Fan Motivation Scale (SFMS) developed in 1995 by Wann tested and proofed empirically the motives of sport fans. These tools includes the eight factors eustress, self-esteem benefits, escape, entertainment, economic factors, aesthetic qualities, group affiliation, and family needs and in total 23 items.[215] The Motivations of the Sport Consumer (MSC) invented by Milne and McDonald (1999) suggested the twelve motivation factors stress reduction, self-esteem, risk-taking, aggression, affiliation, social facilitation, competition, achievement, skill mastery, aesthetics, value development, self-actualization with in total 37 items. The tool attempts to detect the motives why people do sport in general.[216]

---

[212] cf. Mahony et al, 2000, p.24
[213] cf. Choi et al, 2009, p.269
[214] cf. Trail & James, 2001, p.111
[215] cf. Wann, 1995, p.378; cf. Trail & James, 2001, p.112
[216] cf. Milne & McDonald, 1999, p.23-26; cf. Trail & James, 2001, p.112

The final antecedent tool of the MSSC is the Fan Attendance Motivations (FAM) by Kahle, Kambara and Rose described in 1996. This instrument examined the motivation of individuals to attend in college football games. The research focus basically on three motives named emotional connection to team, camaraderie and the importance of winning. In contrast to the SFMS and the MSC the FAM searched not for a specific motive it looks for to which degree the attendance of the games is motivated by the three mentioned motives.[217]

Concluded the MSSC consist out of 32 questions and measures achievement, acquisition of knowledge, aesthetics, drama or eustress, escape, family, physical attractiveness of participants, the quality of the physical skill of the participants and social interaction. The target group of the MSSC were season ticket holders of one specific team of Major League Baseball (MLB). Nevertheless the Motivation Scale for Sport Consumption is adaptable to other teams of different sports. This tool is comparison to its predecessors more confident in validity and reliability.[218]

Another measurement instrument which is invented by Trail et al is the Points of Attachment Index (PAI). The questionnaire published in 2003 is subdivided into 7 categories with 3 items for each which results in 21 questions. The basic categories are identification with the player, with the team, with the coach, with the community, with the sport, with the university and with the level of sport.[219] The second last category shows that the PAI is designed for college sport in north-America.

The last example which will be presented is the Sport Inventory Index (SII) by Funk in 2002. It is a 52 items tool and is constructed to research in specific the woman´s football. The 14 categories with 3 items each are interest in soccer, vicarious achievement, excitement, interest in team, supporting woman´s opportunity in sport, aesthetics, social opportunities, national pride, drama, interest in player, role model, entertainment value, wholesome environment and family bonding.[220]

---

[217] cf. Kahle et al, 1999, p.51; cf. Trail & James, 2001, p.117
[218] cf. Trail & James, 2001, p.118-121
[219] cf. Trail et al, 2003, p.217
[220] cf. Funk et al, 2002, p.33

5   RB LEIPZIG

5.1   HISTORY AND VISION

The club "RasenBallsport Leipzig e.V." was founded in 19th May 2009 by Red Bull.[221] In comparison to north-America the German league system and its teams are not franchises therefore clubs have to be promoted ten times to be allowed to play in the highest division.[222] So that RBL has not start in the lowest league in Germany the playing license for the 5th highest league was paid off by a suburban team called SSV Markranstädt. Further it's not permitted in Germany that the name of the sponsor appears in the naming of a football club. Therefore the club RB Leipzig is pronounced Rasenballsport Leipzig and only the abbreviation leads to the association of Red Bull.[223]

For further understanding a speciality in Germany has to be explained. The DFB decided in 1998 in order to exploit the full marketing potential of professional football that clubs could depart from the traditional club structure. Until then clubs were instructed to be non-profitable. Following this decision, clubs were permitted to move their professional football section into a joint stock company. But to ensure a balanced competition the clubs has to retain the majority shareholding of these joint stock companies (50+1). This additional decision determines that in Germany external companies are not able to take over clubs.[224]

To bypass the regulation of the German law RB Leipzig has still the structures of a traditional club which is defined by the membership scheme. To stay independent also after four years the club consist only out of eleven Red Bull employees. Becoming a RBL member costs 800€ a year with a 100€ first-time registration fee on top. In the meantime and caused by additional requirement of the umbrella organization DFL the club includes 300 members. [225] For comparing the market leader Bayern Munich concludes out of 223.985 members.[226]

---

[221] cf. Merx, 2014
[222] cf. Roschmann, 2013, p.104
[223] cf. Merx, 2014
[224] cf. Schröer, 2009, p.204-205
[225] cf. Oltermann, 2014
[226] cf. Rößner, 2013

After setting the frame and with a 100 million € budget[227] the target of RBL is to reach the first division or to be precise the Bundesliga until 2017. After five years the club promoted already three times and is placed in this season of the second-division on a promotion place.[228] The audience participation is also rising year by year. In the fourth division in average 7.600 fans attend the home games,[229] in the third division already 16.700 fans were coming. At the moment after seven games in the 2nd division the average attendance is 24.700.[230] In the relevant promotion game in May 2013 even 42.700 supporters visited the games against Saarbrucken.[231]

The growing spectator interest stands also in relation with the interest in football of the city Leipzig. Therefore the sponsor has chosen the city deliberately. In addition three facts can be given why Leipzig and football have a strong connection. First, in Leipzig the German football organization DFB was founded in January, 1900. Second, the first winner of the German football championship was named VfB Leipzig. Third, till now the attendance record of Germany occurred at the game between 1.FC Lokomotive Leipzig and Chemie Leipzig 1956 where 100.000 spectators have seen the game.[232]

The recent history from the perspective of football in Leipzig is characterized by inefficient club work. Both teams who were responsible for the attendance record went insolvency. The club Lokomotive Leipzig renamed to VfB even went insolvency twice. Those fans have the image to be political oriented to the right. After starting in 2003 again under the old name in the lowest league they are now playing in the 4th division. The other club BSG merged with Chemie Böhlen to the club called FC Sachsen. As already mentioned this club went also insolvency and was also founded again but in this case two times in 2009. Therefore one club is now called BSG Chemie and the other one is called SG Sachsen. BSG has the image to unite the political left wing and is now playing in the 7th division. SG Sachsen has no clear political orientation and is playing in the 6th division.[233]

---

[227] cf. Merx, 2014
[228] cf. Wöckener, 2014
[229] cf. Ruf, 2013
[230] cf. DPA, 2014
[231] cf. Machowecz, 2014
[232] cf. Mandl, 2014
[233] cf. Dieckmann, 2014

The project RB Leipzig has a lot of opponents especially of fans who belong to clubs who have the image to be traditional. As a result of fan reactions several friendly games for example against Hessen Kassel, Union Berlin, Erzgebirge Aue and Kickers have to be abandoned. Various protests of united fans around Germany takes place to fight against RB Leipzig. The fans who feel offended have the opinion that RBL is destroying football in Germany. On the one hand they believe Red Bull created RB Leipzig just for marketing issues and on the other hand this club is not growing normally and has no tradition. Therefore the rivalled fans express their disgust and call RBL "plastic club"[234] Dietrich Mateschitz, the owner of RBL and Red Bull commented in regard to topic: "The only difference between Barcelona, Munich and Leipzig in 500 years will be that those clubs are 600 years old and we are 500 years old".[235]

Regardless of the correct opinion around Leipzig the football infrastructure is improving in various forms. Through the investments of Red Bull a performance centre worth 35 million € evolves on an area with 100.000 m². The football youth at all ages are promoted with professional support in modern training facilities. Also the stadium in Leipzig is renamed to Red Bull Arena. Beside the style to play is also changed in a way which fits best to the Red Bull image. However further strategic investments are planned for the future. Analysts are expecting that the region around Leipzig will grow from an economic perspective by 200 million €.[236]

Maybe in order to calm down the rivalled and tempered football fans the companies VW and Porsche are supporting RB Leipzig in case of a promotion into the first division. Especially VW possesses the club Wolfsburg as a whole, Bayern Munich to a twelfth and Ingolstadt to a fifth.[237] Because of the geographical link and in regard to Sponsor-Fit the major investment of VW into the club Wolfsburg is perfect. In case of Red Bull who is based in Fuschl, Austria the approach is different. The company Red Bull owns beside of Leipzig clubs in New York, São Paulo and Sogakope (Ghana). The concept of Red Bull is different to conventional sponsoring. [238]

---

[234] cf. Schäfer, 2013
[235] cf. Schumacher, 2013
[236] cf. Merx, 2014
[237] cf. Fritsch-b, 2014
[238] cf. Oltermann, 2014

Instead of marking the helmet of a driver with the company's logo they organize the race. Moreover instead of supporting a club with money in order to improve the game they found the club bring them to the top with the target to become part of the story. The company favourites what is defined as "content marketing".[239]

5.2   SPONSOR IMPACT

The company Red Bull GmbH was founded in 1984 by the Austrian Dietrich Mateschitz and the Thai Chaleo Yoovidhya in Fuschl am See, Austria.[240] Now only 30 years later the brand Red Bull is worth 6.7 billion $ by the ratings of the Forbes list which make them to 74th most valuable brand of the world. With 5.4 billion sold cans of energy drinks in 166 countries [241] and an average of 6.5 country expansion per year the growth is not ending so far. Every year Red Bull is reinvesting one third of their sales again through marketing indirectly into the company which has been 1.4 billion € in 2011.[242] Already the release of the product on the market in 1987 have been given indices that the core competence have been since its foundation the innovative marketing concepts. Within the three years planning time Mateschitz and his former fellow student Kastner designed logo, slogan and design of the can.[243]

Before selling the first product the image of energy drink was constructed in a way to reach young customers.[244] Therefore the brand personality of being cool, rebellious, independent and successful have been promoted consequently from the very beginning till now. Although the brand proposal to get pushed up when drinking was communicated in exaggerated way that it would be even possible to fly. Moreover the brand proposal itself was been formulated as a promise. As one of the first actions the product was proposed as a forbidden drug in order to increase the demand of the target group.[245] The basic concept is unchanged but the way to raise the awareness for the brand have been reached a new level. [246]

---

[239] cf. Oltermann, 2014
[240] cf. Rohrbeck, 2012
[241] cf. Forbes, 2014
[242] cf. Rohrbeck, 2012
[243] cf. Bachler et al, 2012
[244] cf. Rohrbeck, 2012
[245] cf. Fründt, 2010
[246] cf. Bachler et al, 2012

Within the last 30 years a huge network with several representatives has been created all aligned similar to communicate the brand proposal in several ways. To underline the brand personality of Red Bull the company sponsored already in their early years athletes of extreme sport. Afterwards although other different kinds of sports become part of the marketing concept. Now the construct of Red Bull consists out of commitments with racing and football teams,[247] adrenaline sports like skydiving, snowboarding and mountain biking.[248] In the sum 600 athletes had a contract in the year 2012 with the company. According to experts Red Bull have invested around 400 million € in sport in the year 2012 while more than 50% of the investments were fleeting into the formula one teams.[249]

But the marketing construct consists beside of athletes also out of several media instruments like agencies, TV studios, several print magazines and a communications arm.[250] The major difference to typical sport sponsoring is the way of communication. In other words instead of typical co-branding the company banks on the idea to get into the operating business. Instead of being a partner of a sport team or an event Red Bull is the owner and the event operator at the same time. The company is not trying to convince customers of the energy drink but to create a story around the product. Therefore they create huge projects like the jump from the stratosphere to generate awareness of the product, the brand and the logo.[251] Nevertheless the "Project Stratos" was an investment worth 50 million € but the ROI are estimated to be few times higher.[252] The major reason to have such an interconnected system is to create awareness in all possible forms. Beside that marketing actions also feed from a financial perspective the own media facilities the target is to create attention and emotions.[253]

In regard to sport teams and athletes of Red Bull the brand identity and the brand image fits together at every sequent. Fans of such a sport team became indirectly also fans of Red Bull which makes them to internal stakeholder of the brand at the same time. Due to that the fans adapt in affective, cognitive and behavioural way Red Bulls personality.

---

[247] cf. Rohrbeck, 2012
[248] cf. Shapiro, 2012
[249] cf. Bachler et al, 2012
[250] cf. Rohrbeck, 2012
[251] cf. Bachler et al, 2012
[252] cf. Tauber, 2012
[253] cf. Bachler et al, 2012

5.3   RESEARCH DESIGN

For the primary analysis of the research a survey was created which consist manly out of four parts. Although the answers are arranged to the get quantitative sub-results, the whole concept is designed for reaching qualitative results in the end. Due to each part aims to get answers for different topics which are explained in the following.

Because the target group are people who are interested in soccer the survey will be placed in football related surroundings. The beginning question sorts out if the asked person is a fan of RB Leipzig or not. In this way the first and major distinguishing between people who have an affiliation with the club and people who have not are made. Further questions about gender, age, income, education or any other general information are not of interest because they are not relevant for the central research question. In this conclusion the questionnaire should be clear in structure and not overloaded with irrelevant questions. Although only closed questions are used because the secondary analysis perceived already sufficient information for the planned research. It was a target to pack at most 20 questions into the survey which leads basically to several advantages. For the intended eye-on-eye questioning all question fits on one site which is useful for a quick and easy realization and a relieved evaluation later. It is assumed that regardless of the form of questioning the concentration of the respondent will be not overstretched in this way.

In the first part of the survey the Sport Spectator Identity Scale is used (see table 4.2). This socio-psychological tool is relatively short and clear, easy to adjust and offers comparable data. Moreover the degree of identification with RB Leipzig is a central issue here. Therefore the questions are translated and the club name is replaced by RB Leipzig. The respondent persons are offered an 8-point Likert scale.

For the second part of the questionnaire various ideas flow into the chosen questions. First this part attempts to detect the main motive why people support RB Leipzig therefore not all imaginable possibilities have to be questioned. Second the uses of the illustrated tools in chapter 4.4 are critical because there are mainly made for the north-American sport environment and they offer too many questions. Nevertheless the basic concept to look for motives from each of the four categories explained in 4.3 is taken. Third the concept of "basking in reflected glory" may have a special relevance also for

60

several items who a normally affected by them. Out of that considerations a set of 10 questions with two or three items for each group are chosen (see table 5.1).

	Question	Motive	Group
	I support RB Leipzig because		
9	... I can spend time with my friends and family	Community and Family	social interaction
10	... I can be a part of something big	Geographic	
16	... the team plays a really nice football	Aesthetics	
11	... I am out of the region	Vision	involvement opportunity
13	... I am able as an individual to actively promote the fan base	Voice	
17	... the club and the environment offers me great entertainment	Entertainment	perceived value
14	... the club is just different than the others	Distinctiveness	
12	... I like a specific person (management, coach, player)	Team Identification	Achievement Seeking
15	... the main sponsor (Red Bull) stands for quality and success	Sponsor	
18	... I like it to be on the winning side	BIRG and Self-Esteem	

Table 5.1 Questionnaire Structure, 2 nd part, Motivation Scale of RBL fans

One of the most important reason why people attend in games and support a team are explained through their origin. To sort the motive geographic relevance into social interaction is derived from the PAI by Trail. The motive community and family is mainly explainable trough the feminine part of the fans and complete the category social interaction. The next group of motives derived from the idea that people are interested in to destress from daily life. Therefore the items aesthetics, voice and vision form the motive who deals with participating in something. It is noted that the aspect vision is especially invented for this specific case RB Leipzig. To BIRG with a club who will be successful in the future and to participate with them from the very beginning may be a reason for various fans. The next and third category focuses on the perceived value. The highly discussed club in the media combined with the experience in event marketing of the sponsor may present an incomparable factor which attracts also general football fans.

Therefore the motives distinctiveness and entertainment have to be proved. In the last group the directions to connect with something successful will be clarified. It will be tested if the factor self-esteem is attached into a human person like a player or a coach of the club. But also the character of the sponsor which includes being on the top could create a feeling of affiliation. Maybe the main motive is neither the sponsor nor parts of the team maybe it´s just the direct orientation which means it's just the pleasant feeling of being on the winning side. Similar to first subsequent the respondent persons are offered an 8-point Likert scale for each question.

The third block is a single question and is based on the evaluation of Bühler and Scheuermann (see 3.1). It will be tested how fans see the single brand RB Leipzig. Both RB Leipzig and remaining fans can point out their personal opinion regarding the type of brand of RBL. It is assumed that football fans in Germany have a basic knowledge about the character of the five different types (see 3.1), therefore there are not especially explained. In consequence five possibilities to answer are given. In addition also multiple answering is allowed here.

Also the last block is just one question and highlights the considerations of the central research. Just in case people have no attachment to the sponsor by confronting them if the origin is either Leipzig or Red Bull they have to judge. The possibilities to answers are also illustrated on an 8-point Likert scale. But the understanding is in contrast to the first and second questioning part where the lowest number stands for a weak commitment and the highest number is equal for perfect approval. Here the number 1 is to mark if the fans believe in that the origin of the club is the city Leipzig because the club is located there and the sponsor irrelevant. The number 8 is to check if the football interested people have the opinion that the club exists just throughout the sponsor Red Bull and the location is meaningless. The numbers in between corresponds with the respective characteristic. To get comparable data not only RB Leipzig fans as well neutral fans are asked.

To summarize the consideration an overview of the basic structure is given in table 5.2.

Subsequent	Part 1	Part 2	Part 3	Part 4
number of questions	7	10	1	1
Respondent	RB Leipzig fans only		RB fans towards remaining fans	
To detect the...	degree of identification	main motivation for support	Subjective opinion regarding... type of brand	origin

Table 5.2 Basic structure of the research design

5.4   EXPECTED OUTCOME

To make statements for the possible outcome basically the findings of the literature are used. To be more specific each part of the survey will be roughly discussed.

In the first part it is expected to receive similar results as the results shown for Sydney FC.[254] Of course RB Leipzig is not playing in a new created league but the starting point to present professional football after a long time is equal to the situation in Australia. In regard to the sponsor maybe it is comparable to a franchise but maybe it is not therefore different and surprising effects are possible. But however the SSIS may give an insight how intense the affiliation with the club RB Leipzig is for the fans.

To predict the dominant motive depends also on the acceptance in respect of the sponsor. Therefore two ways are possible for the judging behaviour. In the first case the sponsor is perceived like franchises in north-America or Australia which is in comparison to the team rather insignificant. In the second case Red Bull is perceived as something special which would in turn attract many sport fans that have a strong desire to BIRG. However as explained "football first" may occur in the case of Sydney because not even football on semi-professional level was existent.[255] Therefore geographic first and victorious achievement second is expected as the main motives for support of RB Leipzig.

---

[254] cf. Lock, 2009, p.132
[255] cf. Lock, 2009, p.165

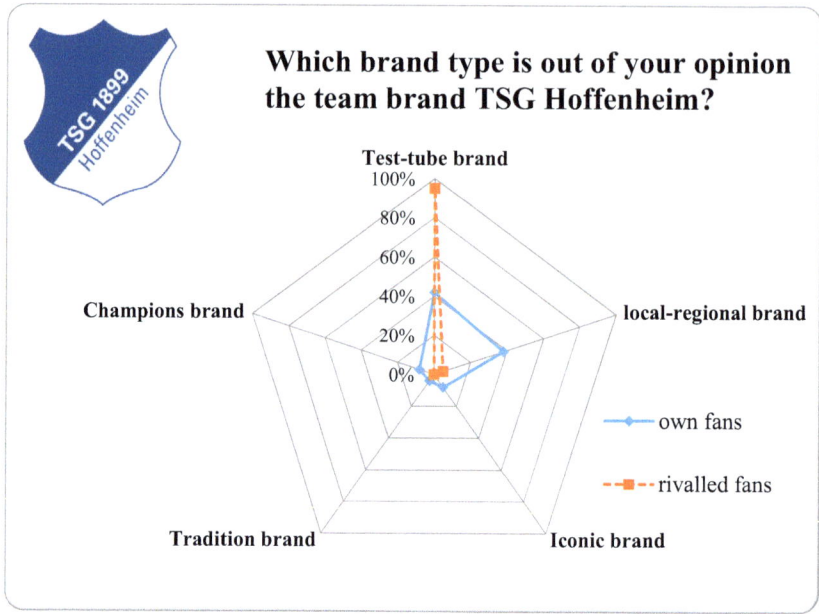

Figure 5.1 Subjective Consideration regarding brand type of TSG Hoffenheim[256], own illustration

In the third part it is more or less expected to receive a brand net which is similar to the brand net of TSG Hoffenheim.(see figure 5.1) The club TSG Hoffenheim is sponsored by a powerful company named SAP and is perceived as the prototype of a test-tube brand. In the case of Leipzig the outcome especially for neutral and rivalled has to be similar but the awareness of Leipzig fans in respect to the own brand is of interest.

The expectation for the last question is similar to the logic of part three. Especially fans who are not affiliated with Leipzig will allocate the origin mainly into the direction of the club. But to confront the fans of RBL that the sponsor possibly created the club leads to unpredictable results. Nevertheless because the city Leipzig is relevant for the existence of the club the result has to be in the balance.

---

[256] cf. Bühler & Scheuermann, 2011, p.46

6 RESULTS

The survey data were collected with two methods. The first method was a face to face interview in form of a questionnaire (see Appendix 1) in an away game of RB Leipzig against the team 1.FC Nuremberg. In this way the attendance of the observed Leipzig fans were already filtered because the interest has to be higher compared to visitors in a home game. But also fans of Nuremberg were interviewed because they consider themselves as supporters of a traditional club and stand for an ideal counterpart to the discussed case. In the second method three different questionnaires (see Appendix 2) were placed online in several football related portals. Due to the polarized perception and the emotional connotation which leads into either supporting or disliking RB Leipzig it was necessary to split the affiliation already in the beginning. In this manner failures through giving wrong statements in a conscious way were minimized.

In the sum 223 people took part in the whole survey. The sample size is composed of 103 football spectators who were interviewed one on one and 120 football supporters who were observed in virtual networks. For each of the four parts various sample sizes exists caused by the incomplete filling in of the questionnaire. Furthermore to improve the efficiency and to make the data more robust a truncated mean is examined for part 1, part 2 and part 4 of the questions. For each part the Windsor mean is calculated by trimming 10% of the values at the beginning and 10% at the end. Moreover all evaluated values were sorted by seize of the mean value.

In the following illustrations the most relevant data are presented. But for the sake of completeness and understanding also the remaining tables are given in Appendix 3. In terms of error analysis for all answers part 1, part 2 and part 4 the mean value, standard deviation, variance, median and the slope are calculated out. A dependence analysis was not examined. To prove the internal consistence a correlation analysis with spreadsheet software was evaluated. The Part 1 shows a Cronbach's alpha of 0,733 and part 2 shows a Cronbach's alpha of 0,728 which is acceptable. But to state and to judge the given results further for each answer a standard deviation and variance of smaller than 2.0 are acceptable. This rule derives from the assumption by taking 25% of the range of values. To guarantee a normal distribution a slope between -0.5 and +0.5 is assumed.

6.1   FAN IDENTIFICATION

In the first part of the survey the psychological commitment of the RB Leipzig fans has been proven. The sport spectator identity scale is by its term normally thought to analyse only the fans in the stadium. Nevertheless the degree of identification is verified of both sport spectators at the stadium and of satellite supporters.

Sport Spectator Identity Scale					
Total (sample size n = 114) ; α = 0,733					
	Mean	StDev	Variance	Slope	Median
Interest in RB Leipzig	7,62	0,61	0,37	0,6	8,0
Importance that RB wins	6,77	1,17	1,37	0,2	7,0
Importance to be a RB fan	6,51	1,16	1,34	0,4	7,0
how Friends see oneself	6,30	1,35	1,82	-0,2	6,0
Awareness of being a RB fan	4,91	2,09	4,38	0,0	5,0
Visual identification	4,48	2,19	4,82	0,2	5,0
distinction to rivals	1,99	1,71	2,92	-0,6	1,0

Table 6.1 Sport Spectator Identity Scale of RB Leipzig fans

Basically the evaluated results showed satisfactory results in regard to all items. The ranking of the most dominant factors are 1.interest in RB Leipzig (7.62±0.61), 2.importance that RB wins (6.51±1.16), 3.importance to be a RB fan (6.30±1.35), 4.how friends see oneself (6.30±1.35), 5.awareness of being a RB fan (4.91±2.09), 6.visual identification (4.48±2.19) and 7.distinction to rivals (1.99±1.71). The first four mentioned aspects resulting in a standard deviation below 1.35 and a variance below 1.82. Also the overall mean above 6.30 confirming a high commitment of the fans with the club.

But the last three aspects deliver some concern which has to be discussed. Both the visual identification with a variance of 4.82 and the awareness of being a RB fan with a variance of 4.38 shows up that the distribution curve is flat. In that case the median and the tendency of the peak are taken into consideration. The rounded up mean values for both are equal with the median. The slope underlines this aforementioned explanation because the values are below 0.2. However the variance which is around 70% of the range of values shows unstable judging. Especially in regard to the visual identification the results between sport spectator and satellite supports varies at the most. For RBL spectators in the stadium it is important to be recognized as a RB Leipzig supporter and shows a mean of 5.73±1.95. Supporters online don't care that much to be observed as fans which results in a mean of 2.90±1.62. Because both values are combined the overall mean is somewhere in the middle and therefore relatively low. For the question regarding 'awareness of being a fan' it was already recognizable in the stadium that people had problems to fully understand that question which lead either to rejection partially or to exaggerating in both directions.

However the question to determine the distinction to rivals is identified as an outlier with a mean of 1.99±1.71. In discovering the reason for this several reasons have been found. The "unfortunate" translation from dislike into hate in the question number seven shows up some asking reactions especially in the discussion boards of the internet. In the stadium one respondent commented: "I don't hate anybody and certainly not another football club". But to relativize the term hate this term is just the increased form of dislike. This in consequence just shifts the whole range into one direction where the value 2 is maybe equal to 5. Therefore another possible cause for this value is maybe just the fact that a relevant rival is not existent. Within the last five years the success in sport of RB Leipzig defocuses the comparison to local clubs in Leipzig because now there are not on the same level of sport anymore.

In comparison with the data of Lock who researched a new football club in Australia the results are very similar (see table 4.1). With except of awareness the order of the aspects are the same. In regard to the cognitive, affective and behavioural factors the fans of Sydney and Leipzig behave similar. But in this correlation here the affective factors like importance that RB wins and being a RB Fan are more dominant than the cognitive factors like awareness of being a RB fan and how friends see one. Likewise the distinction to rivals for the fans of Sydney FC was voted as the lowest dominant factor for identification with a mean of 4.58±2.50.

6.2   MOTIVATION FOR SUPPORT

To dedicate the main motivation the research supported a clear and obvious result. Both the questioning in the stadium and online show those fans defines their origin as the dominant factor for support. In total a mean of 7.47±1.05 and a relatively low variance of 1.09 underline this fact also in numbers. The remaining motives who coming next are

2.entertainment (6.70±1.12), 3.aesthetic (6.68±1.04), 4.distinctiveness (5.70±1.97), 5.community (5.38±1.93), 6.vision (4.97±1.96), 7.victorious achievement (4.26±1.60), 8.voice (4.16±2.13), 9.sponsor (3.78±2.14) and 10.team identification (3.74±1.74) (see table 6.2).

Motivation to Support RB Leipzig					
Total (sample size n=107) ; α = 0,728					
	Mean	StDev	Variance	Slope	Median
Geographic	7,47	1,05	1,09	0,5	8,0
Entertainment	6,70	1,12	1,26	0,3	7,0
Aesthetic	6,68	1,04	1,09	0,3	7,0
Distinctiveness	5,70	1,97	3,90	0,2	6,0
Community	5,38	1,93	3,71	0,3	6,0
Vision	4,97	1,96	3,84	0,0	5,0
Victorious Achievement	4,26	1,60	2,56	-0,2	4,0
Voice	4,16	2,13	4,55	0,4	5,0
Sponsor	3,78	2,14	4,57	0,1	4,0
Team Identification	3,74	1,74	3,01	0,1	4,0

Table 6.2 Motivation to Support RB Leipzig

The three most dominant motives are relatively stable of its value with can be seen in variance and standard deviation which was below 1.27 or rather below 18% of the range. The motivations ranked between 4th and 10th position contain a stronger distribution showing standard deviations between 1.60 and 2.14 and a variance between 2.56 and 4.57. This shows also that fans were not convinced of each reason and answered exaggerating in any direction. Nevertheless to judge the values, the median who expresses the most frequented answer reports equality with the mean values for all items except in case of voice and community. For the latter two we take the slope into the consideration. This parameter that describing if the peak is tending into one direction reports 0.3 and 0.4 and are judged therefore also as sufficient. In addition to that all motives have been proofed as relevant factors.

By comparing the results of the stadium with the online evaluation also various insights are receivable. The mean value of all given answers in the stadium are 1.59 higher than the mean in the internet. Moreover with a mean of 7.92±0.27 the motive geographic in the stadium survey explains that nearly all supporters who attend the away game live in distance to Leipzig or have a strong affiliation with that area. The motive sponsor ranked by spectators of the stadium with 3.68±2.13 on the last position while the online supporters see in the quality of sponsor with 4.00±2.24 the 5th most reason for supporting the club. Due to the characteristic of the respondents the motive community ranked by the stadium attendance with 6.48±1.03 on the 4th position. This stays in contrast to fans in the internet who judge this factor relatively low with 3.33±1.86 and is therefore on position number 8. Regardless if aesthetic is the 2nd most important issue for stadium spectators to support RB Leipzig the dominant motives are geographic, aesthetic and entertainment in both respondent groups. An interesting aspect about fans of RBL is that currently the motives entertainment and aesthetic are stronger for supporting the club than success.

In regard to the sponsor one interviewee answered "I really don't care if it's called Red Bull or Danone Leipzig the most important thing is that we have a successful club in Leipzig." This answer matches with the evaluated results and gives also an impression of the general opinion. The insignificance of winning stays in contrast to the expected results. The relevance for the fans to support RB Leipzig caused by the successes in the youngest history or the expected success in the future is relatively low. Also this impression has been explained while the eye on eye interview: "At the moment it is important that they win but if they have been promoted it's not that important anymore." But on the other side being victorious still is a factor for some parts of the fan base which was commented with the words: "For me it's absolutely important that there is finally a club in East Germany which has the chance to win a championship in the future."

6.3   BRAND TYPE

In the third part of the survey the interest lay in the subjective impression to which kind of brand type RB fans and rivalled fans allocate the team-brand RB Leipzig. The expectation here was a similarity with the given results of Bühler & Scheuermann with the example for Hoffenheim. As expected the self-image of RBL fans differs strongly to the public image of neutral fans or rivalled fans. (See figure 6.1)

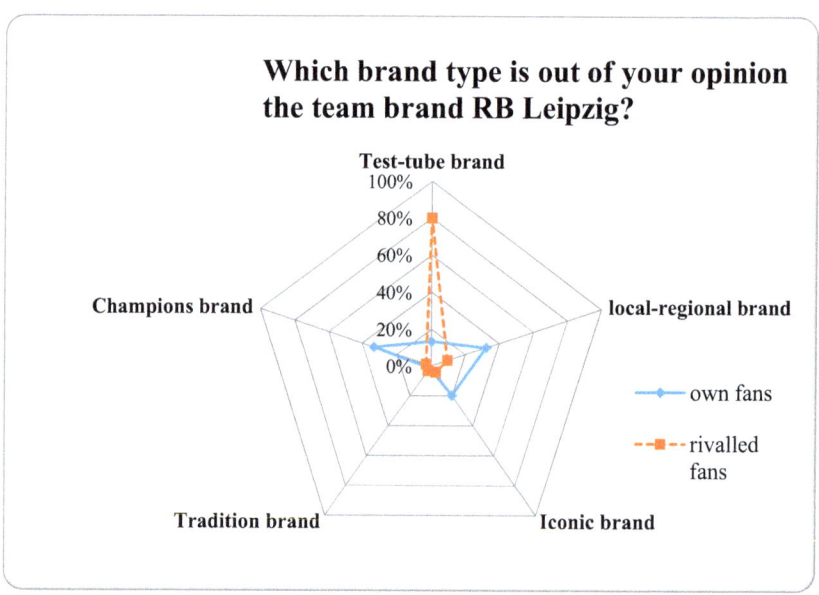

Which brand type is out of your opinion the team brand RB Leipzig?

Figure 6.1 Subjective Consideration regarding brand type of RB Leipzig

Here in total exactly 80% of the rivalling fans considers the single brand RB Leipzig as a test-tube brand. In the stadium this kind of opinion was less pronounced and resulted in two third respectively 65.0%. But in the internet more than 90% of the rivalling fans of RBL consider RBL as a test-tube brand. Moreover the remaining results in regard to the types of brand judged by all rivalled fans are 2.local regional brand with 9.5%, 3.Iconic brand with 4.2%, and tradition brand and champions brand with 3.2% each.

In contrast to the rivalled fans, only 13.1% of the Leipzig fan-base considers the team brand as a test tube one. The dominant opinion here with 33.1% the fans have chosen champions brand close followed by local regional brand with 33.2%. The third most chosen response has been iconic brand with 19.7%. Just tradition brand with 1.6% is ranking clearly on the last position. The greatest difference between online users and spectators who have an affiliation with RB Leipzig was the judgement in either Champions or local-regional brand. For online fans champion's brand (34.4%) is the most reasonable answer but local regional brand has been the top answer for fans of the stadium (37.9%). Only 6.1% of the Leipzig fans in the stadium replied the question with test-tube brand which also indicates the impressions while the questioning.

A few respondent fans of Leipzig consider the question to choose between several types of brands as an affront. The fact that test-tube brand was part of the election was sufficient enough to feel offended. For example one asked back "Do I really have to answer that?" another one crossed out the question and a third one shook annoyed his head while answering. One difference and subjective impression which cannot be underlined in numbers has been observed in the eye-on-eye interview. While nearly all fans of Leipzig who have been asked if they will participate in the survey also agree the fans of Nuremberg were almost difficult to convince.

However the results are explainable with the social identity theory. As determined in the inverted first principle of the SIT, people are not willing to associate the own self-concept with negative connotations. Therefore the negative image which is attended by an artificial created club is rarely a possibility of the own perception. Due to that and because there is a choice one of the alternatives are chosen.

6.4 IDENTITY OF ORIGIN

The last question was in a way a direct comparison if Leipzig or Red Bull is responsible for the formation of the club RB Leipzig. It asked more or less subtle where the origin of RB Leipzig is. In the evaluation some adaptations have been made. Therefore to illustrate the answer better the range of values were shifted into the negative direction. In other words the value 4.5 is the neutral opinion, which is now through the shift equal with 0. Further for the subjective impression of the origin the value -3.5 is equal with Leipzig in contrast to 3.5 which correspond with Red Bull. The answers of the fans each results in different deflection from the neutral perspective show in figure 6.2.

The rivalled and neutral fans determined the origin of RB Leipzig strongly into the direction of Red Bull with a mean of 2.99±1.04. This clear result was expectable and represents the public image of the club at the moment. The online users who have no affiliation with RB Leipzig even rated 3.30±0.4. Also the low variance of 0.16 shows how sharp the opinions have been. Maybe through the discussion the neutral fans in the stadium judged not that precise but still with 2.37±1.77 that RB Leipzig is only existent cause of Red Bull.

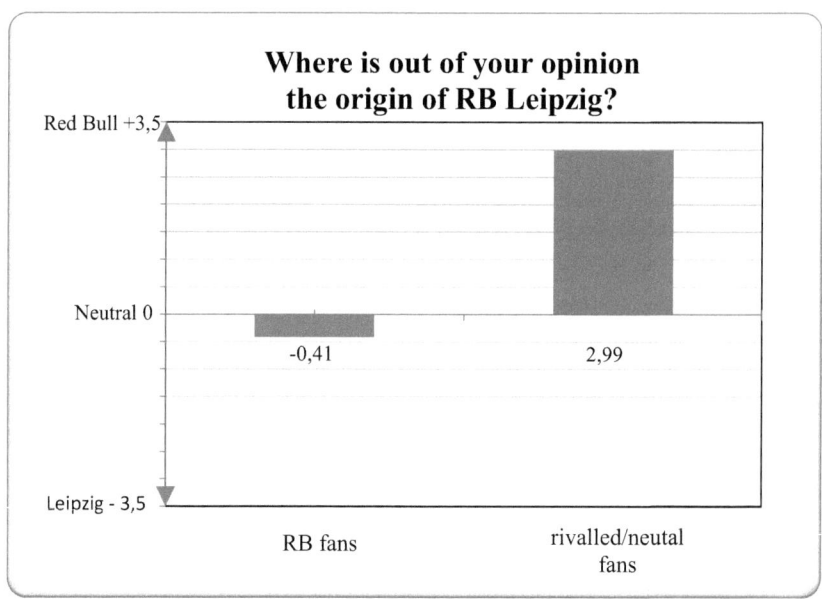

Figure 6.2 Subjective Consideration regarding origin of RB Leipzig

RBL´s own fans of have a different opinion in regard to the formation of the brand RB Leipzig. For them both parties are influential in the evolvement of RBL which results in a mean of -0.41±2.04. The fans of RB Leipzig who took part in the online survey almost voted completely neutral with a mean of 0.01±1.94. The supporters of Leipzig tended to the direction of Leipzig defined with -0.86±2.17.

All parts have shown that RBL fans have a strong identification with the club. But the awareness and existence of the sponsor is partially ignored. Leipzig fans who also attend in a live event show a higher degree of identification than fans in the internet.

7 DISCUSSION AND CONCLUSION

7.1 LIMITATIONS AND FUTURE RESEARCH

The focus now is to judge the research design on correctness, limitations and possible improvement. Despite the sample size was sufficient enough to make qualitative statements but in case for a broader evaluation to sort out by gender, origin or age the number of respondents had reached its limitations.

The degree of identification measured though the SSIS shows only the dimension commitment. The dimension attendance or in other words the frequency of watching games on TV or in the stadium was not covered. Further the question number three of the SSIS was unfortunately translated. The term hate resulted in some confusion which leaded to partial refusal of the whole survey especially in the internet. For this specific question it would be also an advantage to point out one specific team but this was difficult to define. On the one hand local clubs of Leipzig are not on the same level of sport and comparable clubs like Hoffenheim, Leverkusen and Wolfsburg are not accepted from the own fan base as relevant out-groups.

The survey catches up impressions, feelings and psychological connections with the team from several perspectives but to consider one specific aspect in detail the questionnaire was not designed for. This limitation includes also the questions in regard to the main motives supporting RB Leipzig. The result shows dependence to the geographical motivation but to split these further up is not possible. In logical consequence if the identification is city based, region based or based by the former country called GDR was not identified.

Out of the described limitations and consideration several suggestions for future research can be made. The measurements with the SSIS are a snap shot of the present situation but to the see the evolution of the fan base over time regularly measurements have to be done. These would also provide valid and stable data more than the current results because outliers' trough day and match influences would be detected more easily. Also extending and adapting the psychological tool following the model of the PCT will offer better information in regard of classifying the fans.

Corresponding to the suggestions for the SSIS the questionnaire part detecting the motives is improvable. The majority of the respondent named the geographic issues as the main driver for their identification with the club. By examining the survey again with more questions regarding the geographic parameter would provide information to identify the type of the demographic category. Moreover what is the main driver for fans who not grown up or live around Leipzig? Therefore it would be interesting to consider and research the group isolated from the conventional supporters.

Regardless if the survey will be repeated it is proposed to concentrate on only one part of the questionnaire. By extending either block one or block two of the survey the amount of questions would come to a limit in which the questioning procedure reaches a critical point. Already after 20 questions the attention of the respondents seemed to run out. Adapting and applying either the psychological or the motivational part alone brings also the advantage to take gender, age and education into account.

7.2 CONCLUSION AND INTERPRETATION

To sufficient summarize the discussed topic the sub questions of the study's line of action will be answered now. This in turn brings us to the task of discussing the central question.

Which benefits do have sponsors in having a partnership with sport clubs and which forms of implementation do they have?

The major benefit for potential sponsors of advertising with sport is the effectiveness in comparison to the alternatives. Utilizing the sympathy and awareness of football clubs in order to foster the target figures of the own brand is therefore commonly used. Those brand transfer effects are be positively influenced by the amount of placements. Out of that reason buying naming rights of clubs in all forms is the most popular way for companies to increase their sponsoring activation. However through the overload on information the advertising effects becoming weaker in general. Therefore Co-Branding is another form of partnership which is better in facing the change of the society. The basic character is based on the understanding that customers are co-creators of values. Through evaluation together a clear, aligned and jointly message both sponsor and club can gain their brand image and brand awareness more effective and durable.

Which factors influence the brand image in professional team sport and is it possible to influence those factors?

To answer this question the concept of the multidimensional brand management approach of Lane Keller has to be understood. Derived of his explanations a team sport specific model explains that beside of the antecedent awareness the brand image is characterised by the associations the team brand generates. The team brand image is therefore influenced by the associated attitudes, the associations with product-related and non-product-related attributes and the associated benefits. In addition the associated benefits of both symbolic and experiential nature are also mentioned in this context. To change these associations in respective to manage the team brand an improved model has been provided. The identity-based brand management approach understands the brand as a self-reflexive individual with an internal and external image. The consumer observes associations always as a bundle of partial benefits and attributes that are condensed and transformed into one global image. Due to that the proposals of the internal stakeholders are perceived time lagged from the external stakeholders. Therefore the best way to manage the brand is to have a consistent concept from the very beginning which is lived and consumed equally from both brand owners and brand consumers.

What are the strongest and most important reasons in identification for a fan with a professional football club?

The question is targeting on the topic team identification which is basically explainable through the Social Identity theory. Human beings reduce the complexity of the world by comparing, classifying, judging and sorting themselves by. The supreme principle is that each person strives for a positive self-esteem. This concept is observable by fans when they feel affiliated with successful people and when teams represent elements of their identity. Another way to create identification is to involve the fan more in the creating of the core product "event". In this way the fan became indirectly a part of the team. In combination with the consumption theory the constant fulfilling of expectancies fosters identification. It is the thrill of anticipation or the positive feeling being entertained which leads to a strengthened bond between fan and team. In consequence the most dominant factors are origin and success that brings fans to have identification with a professional football team.

Can an identity based team brand be created through a strong sponsor?

The central research question can be answered either from the brand perspective or the degree of affiliation fans have with the club. Nevertheless the answer is in both cases is 'Yes'. From the perspective of brand management the individual character in comparison to other team brands is already determined through the city belonging. The affiliation with the brand is observable through desire of fans to display club related merchandising products like RBL jerseys, scarves and hats. Moreover the huge interest of fans to stay informed in regard to RB Leipzig is an indication that there is a clear expectation in regard to the image of the brand. Through the similarities it is already difficult to draw a clear line between brand and identification. The major difference of those terms is the origin and their derivations. Therefore brands are derived from recall and recognition and the connection to associated benefits and attributes. This stays in contrast to identification which is derived from the social identity theory. The SIT explains that the every person is always striving for a positive self-concept. Fans of Leipzig show an affiliation in cognitive, affective and behavioural way which is only compatible if this affiliation provides a positive self-concept. Therefore there is identification of RBL fans with the club. Nevertheless two remarks shall be given at this point. First the difference in opinion between fans of Leipzig and rivalled fans is perfectly explainable with the SCT. This underlines also the importance for companies to set up prior goals by formulating a vision in order to foster the corporate culture. Second the five stages how new team identification proceeds is an interesting aspect for general marketing how the identification process of customers with a brand could be.

7.3   IMPLICATIONS FOR MANAGEMENT

The study brings various ideas which can be addressed to the management. For example it is necessary to point out the basic identity of RB Leipzig much clearer also in public TV and in the World Wide Web. Maybe picking up some results of the study and propose them as the management concept helps to strengthen the identity and in consequence the brand. The outcome shows a lack in identification with a single people of RBL. For example players who grown up at these region may be highlighted as the representative faces of the club. Moreover the friendly and peaceful interaction may be a positive and typical characteristic for RB Leipzig fans which in addition underlines the difference to local clubs.

In the North-American sport environment useful instruments to improve team identification are already existent. Using the effects of "Basking in reflected glory" by winning the interest of famous people and use them for the own cause. Bring local heroes to watch the game regularly who show recognizable affiliation with RBL in order to encourage others to do the same. But also using fans for the own purpose are reasonable and effective means. Stimulate average identified fans to formulate in public why they are fans. This action takes them on the one side on the own board and on the other side collects arguments for being a RB fan. Further reasonable arguments can be posted via jingles in the home town stadium.

But also to foster the fan community is an important issue. For instance initiate some additional and regular events to address families. Creating child friendly segments in the stadium and winning the heart of football interested kids from the very beginning. Support parents and their children's by offering them friendly modes of transport. Giving the kids little incentives, bring them together with the team and entertain both father and mother. Make the day in the stadium to an incomparable day experience.

But beside of maintaining the brand RB Leipzig a major interest lays also in improving the brand of the sponsor in regard to image and awareness and positive associations. The acceptance of the main sponsor has to be promoted in various forms. The results have shown that the identification with the sponsor is more a form of tolerating than of accepting. Also for this case some useful and brief suggestions can be made. As mentioned already two big sponsors VW and Porsche will also participating in the project RB Leipzig. This in turn could be a also concept for Red Bull by sponsoring traditional clubs like Hamburger SV, VfB Stuttgart or maybe Eintracht Frankfurt to win the general acceptance of football fans in Germany.

Another method to improve the acceptance for the sponsor from all parties is to highlight the positive aspects more in the public communication. The economic benefits of the city Leipzig and the rebellious and creative personality of all brand owners have to be emphasized even more. The needs and desires of fans are taken seriously which stays in contrast to other sponsors. By underlining these habit that the sponsor is really interested in the people would in consequence increase the acceptance for the sponsor.

REFERENCES

Aaker, D.A. (1996). Measuring Brand Equity across Products and Markets, California Management Review, vol. 38, no3, p.102-120

Aaker, J.L. (1997). Dimensions of Brand Personality, Journal of Marketing Research, vol.34, p.347-356

Aleythe, S. (2013). Entwicklung von Rasenballsport Leipzig, Masterplan für den Weg in die Bundesliga, sueddeutsche.de, 6th February 2013 http://www.sueddeutsche.de/sport/entwicklung-von-rasenballsport-leipzig-masterplan-fuer-den-weg-in-die-bundesliga-1.1592716

Alexa, F. (2014). Markenpersönlichkeit von Fußballvereinen, In: Preuß, H., Huber, F., Schunk, H. & Köнеобecke, T. (Hrsg.): Marken und Sport – Aktuelle Aspekte der Markenführung im Sport und mit Sport, p. 167-193, ISBN: 978-3-8349-2751-4, Springer Gabler 2014

Bachler, M. & Gram, M. & Himmelfreundpointner, R. (2012). Red Bull: Der verrückteste Konzern der Welt, format.at, 24th October 2012, http://www.format.at/wirtschaft/business/red-bull-der-konzern-welt-344799

Bauer, H.H. & Stockburger-Sauer, N.E. & Exler, S. (2008). Brand Image and Fan Loyalty in Professional Team Sport: A Refined Model and Empirical Assessment, University of Mannheim, Journal of Sport Management, 2008, vol.22, p.205-226

Bühler, A. & Scheuermann, T. (2011). Marken im deutschen Profisport, der Versuch einer empirischen Klassifizierung, Stuttgart

Bühler, A. & Scheuermann, T. (2014). Kult, Tradition, Champions, lokale Helden und Retorte – Eine empirische Markenklassifizierung im Sport, Preuß, H. & Huber, F. & Schunk, H. & Könecke, T. (Hrsg.) (2014). Marken und Sport, Aktuelle Aspekte der Markenführung im Sport und mit Sport, p.125-143, ISBN: 978-3-8349-2751-4, Springer Gabler 2014

Burmann, C. & Meffert, H. (1996). Identitätsorientierte Markenführung – Grundlagen für das Management von Markenportfolios, Arbeitspapier Nr.100 der wissenschaftlichen Gesellschaft für Marketing und Unternehmensführung e.V. (Hrsg. Meffert, H., Wagner, H., Backhaus, K.), Münster

Burmann, C. & Blinda, L. & Nitschke, A. (2003). Konzeptionelle Grundlagen des identitätsbasierten Markenmanagements, Universität Bremen, Fachbereich Wirtschaftswissenschaft, Arbeitspapier Nr.1

Burmann, C. & Blinda, L. (2004). „Go for Gold" – Fallstudie zum Olympiasponsoring der Bremer Goldschlägerei, Universität Bremen, Fachbereich Wirtschaftswissenschaft, Arbeitspapier Nr.10

Burmann, C. & Schade, M. (2009). Stand der Forschung zum Markenimage professioneller Sportvereine – eine literaturgestützte Analyse unter besonderer Berücksichtigung relevanter Markennutzen, Universität Bremen, Fachbereich Wirtschaftswissenschaft, Arbeitspapier Nr. 40

Burmann, C. & Schade, M. (2010). The brand image of professional sport teams – an analysis of relevant brand benefits and the relevance of brand personality, The Thought Leaders International Conference on Brand Management, Lugano, 18 – 20th April 2010, p.1-13

Choi, Y.S. & Martin, J.J. & Park, M. & Yoh, T. (2009). Motivational Factors Influencing Sport Spectator Involvement at NCAA Division II Basketball Games, Journal for the study of sports and Athletes in education, Volume 3, Issue 3, Fall 2009, p. 265-284

Cialdini, R.B. & Borden, R.J. & Thorne, A. & Walker, M.R., & Freeman S. & Sloan, L.R. (1976). Basking in Reflected Glory: Three (Football) Field Studies, Journal of Personality and Social Psychology 1976, Vol. 34, No.3, p.366-375

Cialdini, R.B. & Richardson, K.D. (1980). Two indirect tactics of image management: Basking and blasting, Journal of Personality and Social Psychology, vol. 39, number3, p.406-415.

Deloitte. (2014). Annual Review of Football Finance. June 2014. Manchester. Deloitte Touche Tohmatsu Limited.

DFL (2013). Bundesliga Report, Die wirtschaftliche Situation im Lizenzfußball, http://www.bundesliga.de/media/native/imported/autosync/report_2013_dt_72dpi.pdf

DFL (2014). Bundesliga Report, Die wirtschaftliche Situation im Lizenzfußball, https://www.bundesliga.de/media/native/dokument/dt_DFL_BL_Wirtschaftssituation_2014_72dpi.pdf

DPA (2014). Für die Bundesliga, Leipzig plant bereits größeres Stadion, t-online.de, DPA, 28th October 2014, http://www.t-online.de/sport/fussball/2-bundesliga/id_71573296/tid_pdf_o/rb-leipzig-plant-bereits-groesseres-stadion.html

Dieckmann, C. (2014). Fußball, Heimat aus der Dose, 17th October 2013 Zeit online, http://www.zeit.de/2013/43/fussball-rb-leipzig-red-bull-bundesliga

FASPO (2012). Sponsor Vision 2012, Trends im Sponsoring-Markt, presentation May, 2012

Forbes (2014). 15th November, 2014, http://www.forbes.com/companies/red-bull/

Funk, D.C. & Mahony, D.F. & Ridinger, L.L. (2002). Characterizing Consumer Motivation as Individual Difference Factors: Augmenting the Sport Interest Inventory (SII) to Explain Level of Spectators Support, Sport Marketing Quarterly, volume 11, number 1, p.33-43

Fritsch, O. (2014). Auch Red Bull fährt jetzt VW, 7th October 2014, Zeit online, http://www.zeit.de/sport/2014-10/rb-leipzig-volkswagen-porsche-sponsoring , Fritsch-b, 2014

Fritsch, O. (2014). WM-Finale: Die Besten im Spiel der Welt, Zeit online, Sport, 14th June 2014, http://www.zeit.de/sport/2014-07/fussball-wm-finale-deutschland-goetze/komplettansicht

Fründt, S., (2010). Dietrich Mateschitz, Der unglaubliche Erfolg des Red-Bull-Gründers, 21st November, 2010, welt.de, http://www.welt.de/wirtschaft/article11092220/Der-unglaubliche-Erfolg-des-Red-Bull-Gruenders.html

Gladden, J.M. &, Funk, D.C. (2001). Understanding brand loyalty to professional sport: Examining the link between brand associations and brand loyalty, International Journal of Sports Marketing & Sponsorship, vol.3, p.67-91.

Gladden, J.M. &, Funk, D.C. (2002). Developing and understanding of brand associations in team sport: Empirical evidence from consumers of professional sport. Journal of Sport Management, vol.16, p.54-81.

Greenwood, P.B. & Kanters M.A. & Casper, J.M. (2006). Sport Fan Team Identification Formation in Mid-Level Professional Sport, European Sport Management Quarterly, vol.6, number 3, p.253- 265

Heere, B. & James, J.D. (2007). Sports Teams and Their Communities: Examining the Influence of External Group Identities on Team Identity, Journal of Sport Management, Vol. 21, 319-337

Jones, I. (1998). Football Fandom: Football Fan Identity and Identification at Luton Football Club, PhD, Luton Business School, University of Bedfordshire,

Kahle, L. R. & Kambara, K. M. & Rose, G. M. (1996). A functional model of fan attendance motivations for college football. Sport Marketing Quarterly, volume 5, number 4, p.51-60.

Kaiser, S. & Müller, C. (2014). Theorie und Praxis der Markenführung im Sport. In: Preuß, H., Huber, F., Schunk, H. & Könecke, T. (Hrsg.): Marken und Sport – Aktuelle Aspekte der Markenführung im Sport und mit Sport, p. 29-44, ISBN: 978-3-8349-2751-4, Springer Gabler 2014.

Keller, K.L. (1993). Conceptualizing, Measuring, and Managing Customer-Based Brand Equity, Journal of Marketing, Vol.57, p.1-22.

Kotler, P.H. (1991). Marketing Management: Analysis, Planning, and Control. 8th ed. Englewood Cliffs, NJ: Prentice Hall

Kerr, A. (2009). "You'll never walk alone" The use of brand equity frameworks to explore the team identification of the `satellite supporter´ Doctoral Dissertation Thesis, University of Technology, Sydney.

Kilian, K. (2014). Prominente Sportler als Testimonials in der Werbung. In: Preuß, H., Huber, F., Schunk, H. & Könecke, T. (Hrsg.): Marken und Sport – Aktuelle Aspekte der Markenführung im Sport und mit Sport, p. 195-213, ISBN: 978-3-8349-2751-4, Springer Gabler 2014.

Kleffmann, G. (2014). Erfolg im Ryder Cup, Und dann macht Kaymer die Säge, sueddeutsche.de, 28th September 2014, http://www.sueddeutsche.de/sport/erfolg-im-ryder-cup-und-dann-macht-kaymer-die-saege-1.2151304

Könecke, T. (2014). Grundlegende Betrachtung des Sports zur Ableitung von Implikationen für das Markenmanagement im und mit Sport. In: Preuß, H., Huber, F., Schunk, H. & Könecke, T. (Hrsg.): Marken und Sport – Aktuelle Aspekte der Markenführung im Sport und mit Sport, p. 45-72, ISBN: 978-3-8349-2751-4, Springer Gabler 2014.

Kolbe, R.H. & James, J.D. (2000). An Identification and Examination of Influences That Shape the Creation of a Professional Team Fan, International Journal of Sports Marketing and Sponsorship, volume 2, number 1, p. 23-37

Linley, M. (2014). City Brandings durch Sport Events. In: Preuß, H., Huber, F., Schunk, H. & Könecke, T. (Hrsg.): Marken und Sport – Aktuelle Aspekte der Markenführung im Sport und mit Sport, p. 235-254, ISBN: 978-3-8349-2751-4, Springer Gabler 2014.

Lock, D. (2009). New team identification: Sydney FC, a case study, Doctoral Dissertation Thesis, University of Technology, Sydney.

Machowecz, M. (2014). RB Leipzig, Wir Ossis brauchen den Retortenverein, zeitonline.de, 9th May 2014, http://www.zeit.de/sport/2014-05/fussball-rb-leipzig-zweite-liga-langfassung/komplettansicht

Madrigal, R. (1995). Cognitive and affective determinants of fan satisfaction with sporting event attendance, Journal of Leisure Research, vol. 27, number 3, p.205-227.

Mahony, F.D. & Madrigal, D.F. & Howard, D. (2000). Using the Psychological Commitment to team (PCT) Scale to Segment Sport Consumers Based on Loyalty, Sport Marketing Quarterly, 2000, volume 9, number 1, p.15-25.

Mandl, D. (2014). Salzburg und Leipzig: Selber Besitzer, selbes Ziel, zwei Herangehensweisen, 30th March 2014, abseits.at, http://www.abseits.at/fusball-business/salzburg-und-leipzig-selber-besitzer-selbes-ziel-zwei-herangehensweisen/

Meenaghan, T. (1991). The role of sponsorship in the marketing communications mix. International Journal of Advertising, volume 10, p.35-47

Merx, S. (2014). Lizenzentzug für RB Leipzig? , Investoren machen den Fussball professioneller, handelsblatt.com, 15th May 2014, http://www.handelsblatt.com/sport/fussball/nachrichten/lizenzentzug-fuer-rb-leipzig-investoren-machen-den-fussball-professioneller-seite-all/9895468-all.html

Milne, G. R., & McDonald, M. A. (1999). Sport marketing: Managing the exchange process. Sudbury, MA: Jones and Bartlett Publishers.

Nößler, R. (2014). Regional Sport, Aufstieg von RB Leipzig treibt Sky-Preise in die Höhe – Kneipen kündigen ihre Pay-TV-Verträge, 14th August 2014, LVZ online, http://www.lvz-online.de/sport/regionalsport/aufstieg-von-rb-leipzig-treibt-sky-preise-in-die-hoehe-kneipen-kuendigen-ihre-pay-tv-vertraege/r-regionalsport-a-250679-print.html

Nufer, G. & Rennhak, C. (2012). Testimonialwerbung mit prominenten Sportlern – eine empirische Untersuchung, Hochschule Reutlingen, Reutlinger Diskussionsbeiträge, Nr. 2012-6

Nufer, G. & Scheurecker, V. (2008). Brand Parks als Form des dauerhaften Event-Marketing, Reutlingen Working Papers on Marketing & Management, Hrsg. Rennhak C. & Nufer, G.

Oliver, R.L. (1993). Cognitive, affective and attribute bases of the satisfaction response, Journal of Consumer Research, volume 20, p.418-430

Oltermann, P. (2014). Why RB Leipzig are sending shockwaves through German football, theguarding.com, 6th March 2014, http://www.theguardian.com/football/blog/2014/mar/06/rb-leipzig-sending-shockwaves-through-german-football

Radler, T.R. (2004). Athletic Bilbao: Das baskische Prinzip, 16th March 2004, Spiegel online, http://www.spiegel.de/sport/fussball/athletic-bilbao-das-baskische-prinzip-a-290094.html

Riedmüller, F. (2014). Marken-Management für Vereine als Ansatz zur Sicherung langfristiger sportlich-wirtschaftlicher Erfolge. In: Preuß, H., Huber, F., Schunk, H. & Könecke, T. (Hrsg.): Marken und Sport – Aktuelle Aspekte der Markenführung im Sport und mit Sport, p. 73-92, ISBN: 978-3-8349-2751-4, Springer Gabler 2014.

Rohrbeck, F. (2012). Red Bull, Ich war eine Dose, zeit-online, number 48, 2012, 1st December, 2012 http://www.zeit.de/2012/48/System-Red-Bull-Sportler-Medienimperium/komplettansicht

Rößner, J. (2013). Kolumne "Auszeit", Warum RB Leipzig nur neun Mitglieder hat, 04th December 2014, welt online, http://www.welt.de/sport/fussball/article122505625/Warum-RB-Leipzig-nur-neun-Mitglieder-hat.html

Roschmann, R. (2013). Zuordnungsprozesse bei Fußballzuschauern, Zur Salienz teambezogener Kategorien, Doctoral Dissertation Thesis, Technische Universität Chemnitz.

Ruf, C. (2013). Drittligist RB Leipzig, Fußball-Party beim Retortenclub, 04th September 2013, Spiegel online, http://www.spiegel.de/sport/fussball/drittligist-rb-leipzig-party-beim-retortenclub-a-920334.html

Schäfer, G. (2013). Frahn: "Wir sind kein Plastik Klub", 17th October 2013, LVZ online, http://www.kicker.de/news/fussball/3liga/startseite/593697/artikel_frahn_wir-sind-kein-plastik-klub.html

Schilhaneck, M. (2006). Markenmanagement im professionellen Teamsport, Sport und Gesellschaft, Jahrgang 3 (2006), Heft 3, 283-305.

Schröer, C. (2009). Profifußball in Europa: Eine Soziologische Betrachtung des Professionellen Clubfußballs in Europa unter besonderer Berücksichtigung Deutschlands und Englands, Doctoral Dissertation Thesis, Universität Osnabrück, Fachbereich Sozialwissenschaften.

Schumacher, M. (2013). RB Leipzig will in die Bundesliga, Schwäbische Bullen, 06th December 2013, stuttgarter-zeitung.de, http://www.stuttgarter-zeitung.de/inhalt.rb-leipzig-will-in-die-bundesliga-schwaebische-bullen.1bfd1bf1-88b0-4926-9f7d-4746f55246f6.html

Selldorf, P. (2013). Fußball Bundesligist Bayer Leverkusen, Mehr als ein Produkt, sueddeutsche.de, 2nd December 2013 http://www.sueddeutsche.de/sport/fussball-bundesligist-bayer-leverkusen-mehr-als-ein-produkt-1.1832864

Shapiro, T.R. (2012). Chaleo Yoovidhya, who made a fortune in Red Bull energy drink, dies in Thailand, 19th March, 2012, washingtonpost.com, http://www.washingtonpost.com/local/obituaries/chaleo-yoovidhya-who-made-fortune-in-red-bull-energy-drink-dies-in-thailand/2012/03/19/gIQANsx6NS_story.html

Snyder, C.R. & Lassegard, M. & Ford, C.E. (1986), Distancing after group success and failure: Basking in reflected glory and cutting off reflected failure. Journal of Personality and Social Psychology, Vol.51, number 2, p.382-388.

Spiller, C. (2014). Bastian Schweinsteiger, Der Boss, Zeit online, Sport, 14th June 2014, http://www.zeit.de/sport/2014-07/schweinsteiger-finale-wm-argentinien/komplettansicht

Sloan, L. (1979). The function and impact of sport for fans: A review of the theory and contemporary research. In J. Goldstein (Ed), Sports, games, and play: Social and psychological viewpoints. New Jersey: Laurence Erlbaum Associates

Tauber, A. (2012), Red-Bull-Gründer, Der Mann hinter dem Sprung durch die Schallmauer, welt.de, 15th October, 2012, http://www.welt.de/wirtschaft/article109853626/Der-Mann-hinter-dem-Sprung-durch-die-Schallmauer.html

Tajfel, H. & Turner, J.C. (1979). An integrative theory of intergroup behaviour. In S. Worchel & W.G. Austin (Eds.), The social psychology of intergroup relations p.33-47. Monterey: Brooks/Cole.

Tajfel, H. & Turner, J.C. (1986). The social identity theory of intergroup behaviour. In S. Worchel & W.G. Austin (Eds.), Psychology of intergroup relations p.7-24, Chicago: Nelson-Hal.

Teixeira, T. (2014). The Brazil World Cup, Big Money for Billions of Eyeballs, Harvard Business School, 12th June 2014, http://www.hbs.edu/news/articles/Pages/big-money-for-billions-of-eyeballs.aspx

Trail, G.T. & James, J.D. (2001). The motivation scale for sport consumption: Assessment of the scale's psychometric properties. Journal of Sport Behaviour, volume 24 number 1, p.108-127

Trail, G.T. & Robinson, M.J. & Dick, R. & Gillentine, A. (2003). Motives and points of attachment: Fans versus spectators in intercollegiate athletics. Sport Marketing Quarterly. Volume 12 number 4, p.217-227.

Trail, G.T. & Anderson, D.F. & Fink, J.S. (2005). Consumer Satisfaction and Identity Theory: A Model of Sport Spectator Conative Loyalty, Sport Marketing Quarterly, 2005, vol.14, number 2, p.98-111.

Trepte, S. (2006). Social identity theory. In J. Bryant & P. Vorderer (Hrsg.), Psychology of Entertainment p. 255-272. Mahwah, NJ: Erlbaum Associates.

Vargo, S.L., Lusch, R.F. (2004). Evolving to a new Dominant Logic for Marketing, Journal of Marketing, Volume 68, January 2004, p.1-17

Wagner, U. & Zick, A. (1990). Psychologie der Intergruppenbeziehungen: Der „Social Identity Approach". Gruppendynamik, 21, p.319-330.

Wagner, U. & Stellmacher, J. (2004). Intergruppenprozesse. In G. Sommer & A. Fuchs (Hrsg.), Krieg & Frieden p.156-168. Weinheim: Beltz-Verlag.

Wann, D.L. & Branscombe, N.R. (1993). Sports fans: Measuring degree of identification with their team. International Journal of Sports Psychology, volume 24, p.1-17.

Wann, D. L. (1995). Preliminary validation of the sport fan motivation scale. Journal of Sport and Social Issues, volume 19, 377-396.

Wann, D.L. (1996). Seasonal changes in spectators` identification and involvement with and evaluation of college basketball and football teams, Psychological Record, volume 46, number 1, p.201-215.

Wann, D.L. & Schrader, M.P. & Wilson, A.M. (1999). Sport fan motivation: questionnaire validation, comparisons by sport, and relationship to athletic motivation, Journal of Sport Behaviour, volume 22, issue 1, p.114-128

Wann, D.L. & Melnick, M.J. & Russel, G.W. Pease, D.G. (2001), Sport Fans. The Psychology and Social Impact of Spectators, Routledge, New York

Wenzel, M. (1996). Soziale Kategorisierungen im Bereich distributiver Gerechtigkeit; Münster; New York; München; Berlin: Waxman Verlag, 1997, Internationale Hochschulschriften, Univ., Doctoral Dissertation Thesis, ISBN 3-89325-496-X.

Wöckener, L. (2014). Geplanter Erfolg, So funktioniert das Fußballimperium von Red Bull, welt.de, 4th May 2014, http://www.welt.de/sport/fussball/article127589372/So-funktioniert-das-Fussball-Imperium-von-Red-Bull.html

Woisetschläger D.M. & Evanschitzky H. & Backhaus C. & Michaelis M. (2009). Trikotsponsoring 2008/09 – Was die Fans der 1. Fußball-Bundesliga über die Sponsoren ihrer Vereine denken, Arbeitspapiere der Juniorprofessur für Dienstleistungsmanagement, Technische Universität Dortmund.

Woisetschläger, D. M. & Backhaus, C. & Dreisbach, J. & Schnöring, M. (2012). Fußballstudie 2012, Wie die Vereinsmarken der Fußball-Bundesliga wahrgenommen werden, Arbeitspapiere des Instituts für Automobilwirtschaft und industrielle Produktion, Technische Universität Braunschweig

Woratschek, H. & Ströbel T. & Durchholz, C. (2014). Sportsponsoring und Co-Branding – innovative Markenstrategien zur Bildung von Allianzen, In: Preuß, H., Huber, F., Schunk, H. & Könecke, T. (Hrsg.): Marken und Sport – Aktuelle Aspekte der Markenführung im Sport und mit Sport, p. 107-123, ISBN: 978-3-8349-2751-4, Springer Gabler 2014.

Zimmermann, J. & Naskrent, J. (2010). Identifikationsstiftende Wirkung des Sportsponsorings. In Sciamus - Sport und Management, 3/2010, p. 48-60.

APPENDIX 1

Survey Eye-on-Eye

1.	Bist du ein Fan, Anhänger bzw. Sympathisant von RB Leipzig?	JA ○	○ NEIN

Fragen 2- 18 nur ausfüllen wenn erste Frage mit JA beantwortet wurde

Wie stark...

1.	siehst du dich selbst als Fan von RB Leipzig?		① ② ③ ④ ⑤ ⑥ ⑦ ⑧
2.	sehen deine Freunde dich als Fan von RB Leipzig?	Gar nicht	① ② ③ ④ ⑤ ⑥ ⑦ ⑧ · sehr stark
3.	hasst du den größten Rivalen von RB Leipzig?		① ② ③ ④ ⑤ ⑥ ⑦ ⑧

Wie wichtig ist es dir...

4.	dass RB Leipzig gewinnt?	nicht wichtig	① ② ③ ④ ⑤ ⑥ ⑦ ⑧ · sehr wichtig
5.	als Fan von RB Leipzig gesehen zu werden?		① ② ③ ④ ⑤ ⑥ ⑦ ⑧

Wie oft...

6.	verfolgst du während der Saison das Geschehen von RB Leipzig (Radio, Fernsehen, Zeitung, Kontakt mit Freunden)?	Niemals	① ② ③ ④ ⑤ ⑥ ⑦ ⑧ · Täglich bzw. Immer
7.	zeigst du in deinem täglichen Leben dass dass du Anhänger von RB Leipzig bist (durch Kleidung, Schal, Trikots)?		① ② ③ ④ ⑤ ⑥ ⑦ ⑧

Ich unterstütze RB Leipzig weil ich...

9.	mit meinen Freunden/Familie Zeit verbringen kann		① ② ③ ④ ⑤ ⑥ ⑦ ⑧
10.	dadurch Teil von etwas sehr Großem sein kann		① ② ③ ④ ⑤ ⑥ ⑦ ⑧
11.	aus der Region komme	Trifft nicht zu	① ② ③ ④ ⑤ ⑥ ⑦ ⑧ · Trifft 100% zu
12.	eine bestimmte Person (Funktionär, Trainer, Spieler) besonders mag		① ② ③ ④ ⑤ ⑥ ⑦ ⑧
13.	als Einzelner die Fan- Gemeinschaft mitgestalten kann		① ② ③ ④ ⑤ ⑥ ⑦ ⑧

Ich unterstütze RB Leipzig weil...

14.	dieser Verein einfach anders ist als die anderen		① ② ③ ④ ⑤ ⑥ ⑦ ⑧
15.	der Hauptsponsor (Red Bull) für Qualität und Erfolg steht		① ② ③ ④ ⑤ ⑥ ⑦ ⑧
16.	die Mannschaft besonders schönen Fussball spielt	Trifft nicht zu	① ② ③ ④ ⑤ ⑥ ⑦ ⑧ · Trifft 100% zu
17.	mir der Verein und das Umfeld hervorragende Unterhaltung bietet		① ② ③ ④ ⑤ ⑥ ⑦ ⑧
18.	es mir gefällt auf der Siegerseite zu stehen		① ② ③ ④ ⑤ ⑥ ⑦ ⑧

		Retorten-marke	Traditions-marke	lokaler Helden	Kult-marke	Champions-marke
19.	Welcher Markentyp ist deiner Meinung nach RB Leipzig?	○	○	○	○	○

20.	Wo liegen deiner Meinung nach die Wurzeln von RB Leipzig?	Stadt Leipzig	① ② ③ ④ ⑤ ⑥ ⑦ ⑧ · Red Bull

APPENDIX 2

Survey Online
Motivational Letter

Hallo zusammen,

im Rahmen einer Studienarbeit führe ich eine Umfrage zur Identifikation bzw. Fanverhalten zum Thema RB Leipzig durch. Ich hoffe der eine oder andere könnte mich dabei unterstützen. Beim Spiel Nürnberg gegen Leipzig habe ich schon erste Ergebnisse erhalten. Wenn sich noch innerhalb der nächsten zwei Wochen so 40-50 Teilnehmer ergeben könnten wäre das eine runde Sache.

Hier die Links:

Als Fan von RB Leipzig bitte
Teil 1 (10 Fragen)
https://de.surveymonkey.com/s/TY23MBB
Teil 2 (auch 10 Fragen)
https://de.surveymonkey.com/s/TC966HX
anklicken

Als Gegner bzw. neutrale Person bitte bei folgender Umfrage mitmachen (sind nur 2 Fragen)
https://de.surveymonkey.com/s/TX83KK9

Vielen Dank schon mal
Ich hoffe die Links funktionieren

Visualization

As a fan of RB Leipzig (Part 1)

Page 1

25%

*1. Bist du ein Fan, Anhänger bzw. Sympathisant von RB Leipzig?

⃝ Ja   ⃝ Nein

[Weiter]

Page 2

Fanbefragung RB Leipzig Teil 1

Fanbefragung

50%

*2. Wie stark siehst du dich selbst als Fan von RB Leipzig?

Gar nicht 1	2	3	4	5	6	7	sehr stark 8
⃝	⃝	⃝	⃝	⃝	⃝	⃝	⃝

*3. Wie stark sehen deine Freunde dich als Fan von RB Leipzig?

Gar nicht 1	2	3	4	5	6	7	sehr stark 8
⃝	⃝	⃝	⃝	⃝	⃝	⃝	⃝

*4. Wie stark hasst du den größten Rivalen von RB Leipzig?

Gar nicht 1	2	3	4	5	6	7	sehr stark 8
⃝	⃝	⃝	⃝	⃝	⃝	⃝	⃝

[Zurück] [Weiter]

Page 3

Fanbefragung RB Leipzig Teil 1

75%

*5. Wie wichtig ist es dir, dass RB Leipzig gewinnt?

nicht wichtig 1	2	3	4	5	6	7	sehr wichtig 8
⃝	⃝	⃝	⃝	⃝	⃝	⃝	⃝

*6. Wie wichtig ist es dir als Fan von RB Leipzig gesehen zu werden?

nicht wichtig 1	2	3	4	5	6	7	sehr wichtig 8
⃝	⃝	⃝	⃝	⃝	⃝	⃝	⃝

*7. Wie oft verfolgst du während der Saison das Geschehen von RB Leipzig (Radio, Fernsehen, Zeitung, Kontakt mit Freunden)?

Niemals 1	2	3	4	5	6	7	Täglich/Immer 8
⃝	⃝	⃝	⃝	⃝	⃝	⃝	⃝

*8. Wie oft zeigst du in deinem täglichen Leben, dass du Anhänger von RB Leipzig bist (durch Kleidunng, Schal, Trikots)?

Niemals 1	2	3	4	5	6	7	Täglich/Immer 8
⃝	⃝	⃝	⃝	⃝	⃝	⃝	⃝

[Zurück] [Weiter]

Page 4

100%

9. Welcher Markentyp ist deiner Meinung nach RB Leipzig?

Retortenmarke	Traditionsmarke	lokal-regionale Marke	Kultmarke	Championsmarke
○	○	○	○	○

* 10. Wo liegen deiner Meinung nach die Wurzeln von RB Leipzig?

Stadt Leipzig 1	2	3	4	5	6	7	Red Bull 8
○	○	○	○	○	○	○	○

Vielen Dank für die Mitarbeit

As a fan of RB Leipzig (Part 2)

Page 1

50%

* 1. Ich unterstütze RB Leipzig weil ich ...
mit meinen Freunden/Familie Zeit verbringen kann?

Trifft nicht zu 1	2	3	4	5	6	7	Trifft 100% zu 8
○	○	○	○	○	○	○	○

* 2. Ich unterstütze RB Leipzig weil ich ...
dadurch Teil von Etwas sehr Großem sein kann

Trifft nicht zu 1	2	3	4	5	6	7	Trifft 100% zu 8
○	○	○	○	○	○	○	○

* 3. Ich unterstütze RB Leipzig weil ich ...
aus der Region komme

Trifft nicht zu 1	2	3	4	5	6	7	Trifft 100% zu 8
○	○	○	○	○	○	○	○

* 4. Ich unterstütze RB Leipzig weil ich ...
eine bestimmte Person (Funktionär, Trainer, Spieler) besonders mag

Trifft nicht zu 1	2	3	4	5	6	7	Trifft 100% zu 8
○	○	○	○	○	○	○	○

* 5. Ich unterstütze RB Leipzig weil ich ...
als Einzelner die Fan-Gemeinschaft mitgestalten kann

Trifft nicht zu 1	2	3	4	5	6	7	Trifft 100% zu 8
○	○	○	○	○	○	○	○

Weiter

Page 2

100%

* 6. Ich unterstütze RB Leipzig weil...
dieser Verein einfach anders ist als die Anderen

Trifft nicht zu 1	2	3	4	5	6	7	Trifft 100% zu 8
○	○	○	○	○	○	○	○

* 7. Ich unterstütze RB Leipzig weil...
der Hauptsponsor (Red Bull) für Qualität und Erfolg steht

Trifft nicht zu 1	2	3	4	5	6	7	Trifft 100% zu 8
○	○	○	○	○	○	○	○

* 8. Ich unterstütze RB Leipzig weil...
die Mannschaft besonders schönen Fussball spielt

Trifft nicht zu 1	2	3	4	5	6	7	Trifft 100% zu 8
○	○	○	○	○	○	○	○

* 9. Ich unterstütze RB Leipzig weil...
mir der Verein und das Umfeld hervorragende Unterhaltung bietet

Trifft nicht zu 1	2	3	4	5	6	7	Trifft 100% zu 8
○	○	○	○	○	○	○	○

* 10. Ich unterstütze RB Leipzig weil...
es mir gefällt auf der Siegerseite zu stehen

Trifft nicht zu 1	2	3	4	5	6	7	Trifft 100% zu 8
○	○	○	○	○	○	○	○

Zurück   Fertig

As a rival of RB Leipzig or neutral fan

Page 1

Fanbefragung zu RB Leipzig

50%

*1. Bist du ein Fan, Anhänger bzw. Sympathisant von RB Leipzig?

○ Ja   ○ Nein

Weiter

Page 2

Fanbefragung zu RB Leipzig

100%

2. Welcher Markentyp ist deiner Meinung nach RB Leipzig?

Retortenmarke	Traditionsmarke	lokal-regionale Marke	Kultmarke	Championsmarke
○	○	○	○	○

*3. Wo liegen deiner Meinung nach die Wurzeln von RB Leipzig?

Stadt Leipzig 1	2	3	4	5	6	7	Red Bull 8
○	○	○	○	○	○	○	○

Vielen Dank für die Mitarbeit

Answering Behavior

As a fan of RB Leipzig (Part 1)

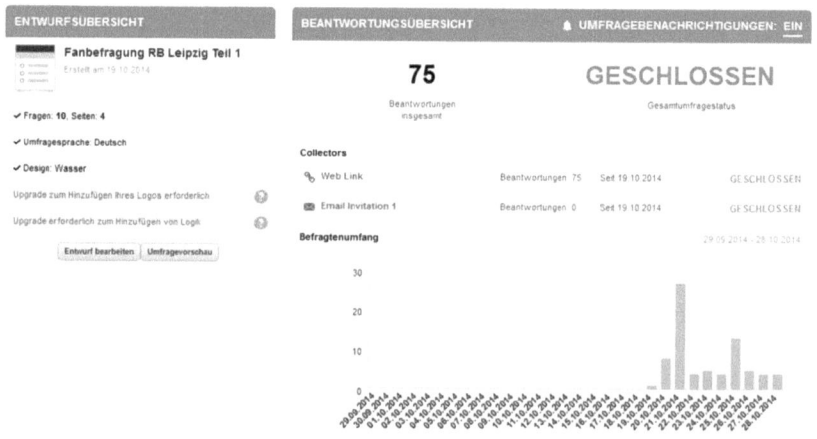

ENTWURFSÜBERSICHT

Fanbefragung RB Leipzig Teil 1
Erstellt am 19.10.2014

✓ Fragen: 10, Seiten: 4

✓ Umfragesprache: Deutsch

✓ Design: Wasser

Upgrade zum Hinzufügen Ihres Logos erforderlich

Upgrade erforderlich zum Hinzufügen von Logit

Entwurf bearbeiten   Umfragevorschau

BEANTWORTUNGSÜBERSICHT   🔔 UMFRAGEBENACHRICHTIGUNGEN: EIN

75   **GESCHLOSSEN**

Beantwortungen   Gesamtumfragestatus
insgesamt

Collectors

🔗 Web Link   Beantwortungen: 75   Seit 19.10.2014   GESCHLOSSEN

✉ Email Invitation 1   Beantwortungen: 0   Seit 19.10.2014   GESCHLOSSEN

Befragtenumfang   29.09.2014 - 28.10.2014

As a fan of RB Leipzig (Part 2)

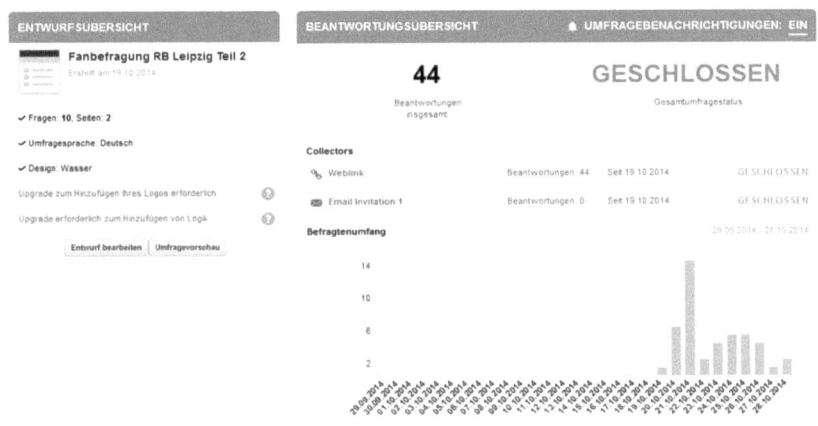

As a rival of RB Leipzig or neutral fan

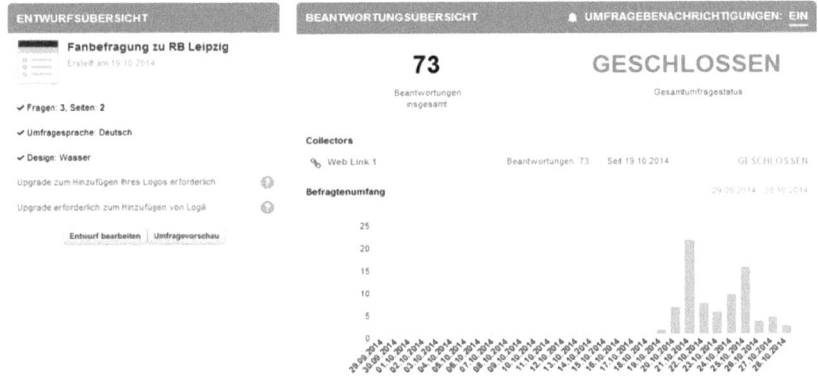

APPENDIX 3

RESULTS – A

Sport Spectator Identity Scale					
Total (sample size n = 114); α = 0,733					
	Mean	StDev	Variance	Slope	Median
Interest in RB Leipzig	**7,62**	0,61	0,37	0,6	8,0
Importance that RB wins	**6,77**	1,17	1,37	0,2	7,0
Importance to be a RB fan	**6,51**	1,16	1,34	0,4	7,0
how Friends see oneself	**6,30**	1,35	1,82	-0,2	6,0
Awareness of being a RB fan	**4,91**	2,09	4,38	0,0	5,0
Visual identification	**4,48**	2,19	4,82	0,2	5,0
distinction to rivals	**1,99**	1,71	2,92	-0,6	1,0

Sport Spectator Identity Scale					
stadium (sample size n = 64); α = 0,697					
	Mean	StDev	Variance	Slope	Median
Interest in RB Leipzig	**7,83**	0,38	0,15	0,5	8,0
Importance that RB wins	**7,15**	1,09	1,19	0,8	8,0
Importance to be a RB fan	**7,02**	1,06	1,12	0,0	7,0
how Friends see oneself	**6,90**	1,14	1,30	0,1	7,0
visual identification	**5,73**	1,95	3,81	0,1	6,0
Awareness of being a RB fan	**5,65**	2,01	4,03	0,2	6,0
distinction to rivals	**2,35**	2,09	4,35	-0,6	1,0

Sport Spectator Identity Scale					
online (sample size n = 50); α = 0,657					
	Mean	StDev	Variance	Slope	Median
Interest in RB Leipzig	**7,21**	0,95	0,90	0,3	7,5
Importance that RB wins	**6,19**	1,21	1,48	-0,2	6,0
Importance to be a RB fan	**5,64**	1,30	1,70	0,3	6,0
how Friends see oneself	**5,33**	1,51	2,28	0,4	6,0
Awareness of being a RB fan	**3,93**	1,90	3,63	0,0	4,0
visual identification	**2,90**	1,62	2,62	-0,6	2,0
distinction to rivals	**1,57**	1,15	1,32	-0,5	1,0

RESULTS – B

Motivation to Support RB Leipzig					
Total (sample size n=107); α = 0,728					
	Mean	StDev	Variance	Slope	Median
Geographic	**7,47**	1,05	1,09	0,5	8,0
Entertainment	**6,70**	1,12	1,26	0,3	7,0
Aesthetic	**6,68**	1,04	1,09	0,3	7,0
Distinctiveness	**5,70**	1,97	3,90	0,2	6,0
Community	**5,38**	1,93	3,71	0,3	6,0
Vision	**4,97**	1,96	3,84	0,0	5,0
Victorious Achievement	**4,26**	1,60	2,56	-0,2	4,0
Voice	**4,16**	2,13	4,55	0,4	5,0
Sponsor	**3,78**	2,14	4,57	0,1	4,0
Team Identification	**3,74**	1,74	3,01	0,1	4,0

Motivation to Support RB Leipzig					
stadium (sample size n=64); α = 0,677					
	Mean	StDev	Variance	Slope	Median
Geographic	**7,92**	0,27	0,08	0,3	8,0
Aesthetic	**7,18**	0,80	0,64	-0,2	7,0
Entertainment	**7,08**	0,99	0,97	-0,1	7,0
Community	**6,48**	1,03	1,07	-0,5	6,0
Distinctiveness	**6,36**	1,61	2,60	0,4	7,0
Vision	**5,64**	1,79	3,21	0,2	6,0
Voice	**5,14**	1,84	3,39	0,2	5,5
Victorious Achievement	**4,54**	1,16	1,36	-0,5	4,0
Team Identification	**4,18**	1,84	3,38	-0,1	4,0
Sponsor	**3,68**	2,13	4,55	0,2	4,0

Motivation to Support RB Leipzig					
online (sample size n=43); α = 0,650					
	Mean	StDev	Variance	Slope	Median
Geographic	**6,41**	1,72	2,94	0,3	7,0
Entertainment	**5,74**	1,43	2,05	0,2	6,0
Aesthetic	**5,44**	1,15	1,33	0,5	6,0
Distinctiveness	**4,41**	2,14	4,56	0,3	5,0
Sponsor	**4,00**	2,24	5,00	0,0	4,0
Victorious Achievement	**3,78**	2,19	4,79	0,1	4,0
Vision	**3,70**	1,84	3,37	-0,4	3,0
Community	**3,33**	1,86	3,46	-0,2	3,0
Team Identification	**3,07**	1,62	2,61	0,0	3,0
Voice	**2,41**	1,53	2,33	-0,3	2,0

RESULTS – C

Which brand type is out of your opinion the team brand RB Leipzig?

rivalled/neutral fans			
sample size	39	55	**94**
	stadium	online	**Total**
Test-tube brand	65,0%	90,9%	**80,0%**
local-regional brand	22,5%	0,0%	**9,5%**
Iconic brand	5,0%	3,6%	**4,2%**
Tradition brand	2,5%	3,6%	**3,2%**
Champions brand	5,0%	1,8%	**3,2%**

RB fans			
sample size	64	61	**125**
	stadium	online	**Total**
Champions brand	31,8%	34,4%	**33,1%**
local-regional brand	37,9%	26,2%	**32,3%**
Iconic brand	24,2%	14,8%	**19,7%**
Test-tube brand	6,1%	21,3%	**13,4%**
Tradition brand	0,0%	3,3%	**1,6%**

RESULTS – D

Where is out of your opinion the origin of RB Leipzig?

total (sample size n = 223)					
	Mean	STDEV	Variance	Slope	Median
RB fans (n = 127)	**-0,41**	2,04	4,18	0,0	-0,5
rivalled/neutral fans (n = 96)	**2,99**	1,04	1,08	0,5	3,5

stadium (sample size n = 103)					
	Mean	STDEV	Variance	Slope	Median
RB fans (n = 64)	**-0,86**	2,17	4,70	0,2	-0,5
rivalled/neutral fans (n = 39)	**2,37**	1,77	3,12	0,6	3,5

online (sample size n = 120)					
	Mean	STDEV	Variance	Slope	Median
RB fans (n = 63)	**0,01**	1,94	3,77	-0,3	-0,5
rivalled/neutral fans (n = 57)	**3,30**	0,40	0,16	0,5	3,5